HUMAN DESIGN MADE SIMPLE

EMMA DUNWOODY

T0368841

RIDER

1

Rider, an imprint of Ebury Publishing
20 Vauxhall Bridge Road
London SW1V 2SA

Rider is part of the Penguin Random House group of companies
whose addresses can be found at global.penguinrandomhouse.com

First published by Rider in 2024

www.penguin.co.uk

A CIP catalogue record for this book is available from the British Library

ISBN 9781846048265

Typeset in 11/17.3pt Adobe Caslon Pro by Jouve (UK), Milton Keynes
Printed and bound in Great Britain by Clays Ltd, Elcograf S.p.A.

The authorised representative in the EEA is Penguin Random House Ireland,
Morrison Chambers, 32 Nassau Street, Dublin D02 YH68

Penguin Random House is committed to a sustainable future
for our business, our readers and our planet. This book is made
from Forest Stewardship Council® certified paper.

For Cooper and Oscar, and all those desiring a life of freedom and authenticity.

CONTENTS

Part 3 – Bringing it All Together

Appendices

INTRODUCTION

Hello, beautiful human . . .

Are you ready to win at the game of life? If the answer is 'yes', it's time to throw out the rules you've been following and pursue a different playbook . . . one that was tailor-made for you, to help you get down to the business of being the best and most authentic version of you: your Human Design.

Human Design is a system that brings together ancient spiritual wisdom and modern scientific knowledge to rewrite the rules of success, abundance, purpose, love and life so that *everyone* is empowered to thrive.

The journey to understanding your Human Design begins when you generate a chart that draws on the time and location of your birth to map out a detailed picture of:

- Your most authentic self.
- The specific potential that lies within you.
- The purpose you're here to fulfil.
- What superpowers and tools you have at your disposal.

- How you're designed to succeed, and to attract money, love, happiness and fulfilment.
- How you can take actions, make decisions and pursue people and environments that will move you towards the beautiful, fulfilling life you were Designed – and deserve – to live.

GENERATE YOUR FREE HUMAN DESIGN CHART NOW

www.emmadunwoody.com

MY HUMAN DESIGN JOURNEY

My path into Human Design started in a doctor's office 20 years ago, when I was diagnosed with depression and panic disorder. This news was devastating. Even more upsetting was my doctor's prognosis that I would never heal – that the best I could hope for was to learn how to manage this condition for the rest of my life.

That was a defining moment for me, because managing it wasn't good enough. I was living with too much pain to accept that it would be part of my life forever. I had to do better than what that doctor said was possible. So, I walked out of that appointment with a mission: I was going to find my own way to heal.

The happy ending is that with time, determination and faith in my ability to do better than simply manage, I *did* do better. I *got* better. And healing my mind and heart was only the beginning of tapping into my full potential.

For the next two decades, I dedicated myself to the science of happiness and success, to the study of the human brain and human behaviour.

What I learned not only healed my mental health, it gave me the tools I needed to make hard decisions for my own happiness and success, like leaving a soul-destroying career in advertising, moving cities, certifying as a Master Coach, starting my own business and transforming my relationships with family.

Over the course of my quest to heal, understand human behaviour and help the people I worked with in my growing coaching business, I discovered Human Design: a life-changing tool for understanding yourself at the deepest level, and experimenting with the elements that make you you, to create the beautiful, meaningful life you are Designed – and deserve – to live.

Now, I'd be lying if I said that my first experience with Human Design was an epiphany. The truth is that, at first, I found it hard to understand and full of negative, disempowering language.

But Human Design just wouldn't leave me alone – it kept nudging its way into my life, and even though I struggled to accept it at first, I couldn't deny that I was curious. I thought: what if I *could* find a simpler, more positive way into Human Design, a way of thinking about this complex system that could feel inviting instead of overwhelming, empowering instead of dogmatic? Some gut-level niggle told me that the keys to my kingdom were waiting in the realm of Human Design – I just had to find my way there.

And then, I did.

I found out that one of Australia's leading Human Design experts lived a stone's throw away from my own home in Sydney, and her approach was much more in line with the kind of experience I was looking for. So I went all in – I reached out and began an experiment to find my own path to understanding and working with my Design.

I started by experimenting with the two most foundational elements of my Design: my Strategy and Authority. (You'll learn more about your own Strategy and Authority in Part 2 of this book.) My Strategy showed me that I thrive when I *respond to* opportunities that are already present in my life, rather than chasing down work. I freed myself from the pressure to be constantly initiating projects, and as a result found myself working less and achieving more ease and flow in my life.

Then I started experimenting with making decisions in line with my Emotional Authority, which empowered me to slow down and sleep on things before giving myself or others an answer straight away. I noticed I was saying 'no' more often, which meant that the things I *did* say 'yes' to were things I really loved, instead of things I felt expected to do in order to please other people.

Following my Strategy and Authority transformed my work and relationships. I followed their guidance in my business, and transitioned from living paycheque to paycheque to running a successful business that supports my family.

And speaking of my family: allowing Human Design principles to influence my parenting approach has opened up so many opportunities for me to better guide and empower my children.

I regularly look to my kids' Designs for guidance on how to be the best mum for them. Knowing how they're both Designed to learn, I've shared with them about how their specific energy works and how to manage it. I understand exactly how they need to feel to be the most encouraged, and I know what they need when they're feeling lost or challenged.

In a time when depression, anxiety and suicide are at an all-time high for young people, I know that my kids are equipped with the tools they need to care for themselves as they navigate challenges, and the elements of their Design help them to practise and build self-compassion and resilience.

Embracing Human Design has shown me that we're not all meant to operate the same way, which is why following other people's advice or path to success rarely achieves the desired effect. It's taught me that we are each a perfectly Designed piece of a bigger cosmic puzzle and the most powerful thing we can do is unlock our inner wisdom, let go of the expectations society places on us and leave the path of conformity to become our truest selves.

Since learning about, understanding and working with my Human Design, I've been able to build the kind of life I always dreamed of living but couldn't create for myself.

Today, I run a successful global business helping people from all over the world discover and activate their potential and access their greatest success, by their own definition, in all areas of their lives. I have a work schedule that's built around my passions and my preferences – I work three days a week and spend the rest of my time doing things I love, like spending time adventuring with my family, travelling and riding my Dressage horse, Legacy.

Through the deep self-knowledge that Human Design provides, I'm armed with all the tools I need to navigate change, challenges, new opportunities and desires in a way that feels authentic, energetically supportive and life-giving to me. I am deeply confident in my ability to navigate anything life throws at me.

Human Design has been the road map – no, the treasure map that has unlocked my most authentic, magical self.

Now I want to share that map with you through this book – it's the resource I wish I'd had when I first encountered Human Design years ago.

My path into Human Design was long and complicated. But yours doesn't have to be.

Your Human Design journey can be simple, straightforward and soul-supporting from the very start. This book is here to help, and to keep you company along the way.

HOW TO USE THIS BOOK

This book was created to do exactly what it says on the cover: make Human Design simple. That's no easy task for a system that includes hundreds of components and synthesises thousands of years of wisdom and science into complex, individual energetic maps.

But together, you and I are going to make it happen. Over the course of this book, I'm going to break down everything you need to know about Human Design into digestible, easy-to-follow explanations and advice – and you are going to lean in, trust the process and learn at your own pace.

EMBRACE THE EXPERIMENT

This book is not a textbook. It's a field guide, designed to help you walk through the world, not pass some imaginary test. To make the most of what's here, you need to approach your Human Design journey as an experiment. That means there will be things that work for you and things that don't. It means some of the things that work for you now won't work for you later, and vice versa. It means you get to creatively adapt the knowledge and suggestions in this book in whatever way feels good, authentic and in Alignment for you.

The object of the game is to have fun and discover what is true for you, to uncover your most authentic self – that is, who you really are at your core, not who the world has told you it's acceptable to be.

Uncovering your authentic self doesn't happen overnight; your life probably isn't going to immediately change the first time or even the second time you experiment with your Design. What *will* change your life is a long-term commitment to experimenting with and growing into your Design, piece by piece.

YOUR HUMAN DESIGN JOURNEY

In these pages, you'll find:

- Everything you need to wrap your head around how Human Design works and why.
- Detailed step-by-step guidance on the major components of your Design: your Type, Strategy, Authority and Profile.
- Actionable tips on applying your new self-knowledge to your everyday life.
- Plus extra resources delving more deeply into your Design once you've mastered the basics.

KEEP A JOURNAL

I recommend keeping a journal throughout your process with this book, so that you can track what resonates and feels true to you as you begin your own unique Human Design experiment.

Finally, before we go any further, I want you to remember: this book was created to simplify your Human Design experience. The operative word in that sentence is *your*. The journey *you'll* go on with this book and with *your* relationship to Human Design is *yours*, so trust yourself through this process. Pay attention to what feels true and helpful and authentic to you. Don't look to this book as a set of rules you have to follow; look to it instead as a series of signposts that can help you find your own way, write your own rules and ultimately unlock the door to *your* authenticity and greatness . . . *your* unique journey with Human Design.

PART 1

KEY CONCEPTS MADE SIMPLE

1.
WHAT IS HUMAN DESIGN?

Human Design is a system that brings together ancient spiritual wisdom with modern scientific knowledge to rewrite the rules when it comes to success, abundance, purpose, love and life so that *everyone* is empowered to thrive. Human Design as we know it today was introduced to the world by a spiritual guru called Ra Uru Hu in the 1980s, and draws upon four ancient wisdoms.

WESTERN ASTROLOGY

Astrology can help you understand your place in this world by mapping your unique connection to the movements of the celestial bodies.

Astrologers believe that when you possess the knowledge of how the Universe influences you, you get to decide how to work with that instead of against it – Human Design experts know this to be true, too.

Like your astrological birth chart, your Design is based on where the celestial bodies were in the sky at the time of your birth. But a Human Design chart can take you further than your astrology, because in addition to looking at what was happening in the sky at the time of your *birth*, your Human Design takes into account the celestial events of a major moment *in utero* – the moment your soul entered the body three months before you were born.

THE CHAKRA SYSTEM

Rooted in Hindu and Buddhist traditions, the Chakra system charts the energetic centres of the body. Traditionally, the Chakra system focuses on seven main Chakras, running down the spine (Crown, Third Eye or Mind, Throat, Heart, Solar Plexus, Sacral and Root). Human Design expands that list of energetic Centres from seven to nine, adding the Splenic Centre and splitting the Heart Chakra into two: the G Centre and the Heart, Ego or Will Centre).

You'll learn more about the Centres on page 41.

THE KABBALISTIC TREE OF LIFE

The Tree of Life, which originates in Judeo-Christian mystic traditions, is an ancient symbol for how the Universe was – and how energy continues to be – created. Over time, the Tree of Life diagram also became associated with spiritual and energetic evolution on a more individual level.

The Tree consists of ten nodes, representing spiritual and energetic stages, or the pit stops along the path to spiritual and energetic enlightenment. These nodes are connected by lines that represent the process of moving from one stage to the next.

Human Design maps an energetic movement and evolution that is similar to what we see represented in the Tree of Life. In your Human Design chart, you'll see lines connecting your energetic Centres to each other – we call these Channels and, like the lines in the Tree of Life, they communicate the way that energy moves from place to place in your body and your aura.

THE I CHING

The I Ching is a Chinese text that dates back to the eighth century BC. Its name translates to 'Book of Changes' – so, like the Chakra system and the Tree of Life, it charts energetic change and evolution.

According to the I Ching, human beings are capable of 64 distinct types of transformation, known as Hexagrams.

Your Human Design chart features 64 Hexagrams, too – we call them Gates. Gates are the points of entry and exit into each energetic Centre, and they function differently for every individual. You can learn more about Gates on page 268.

Sixty-four also happens to be the number of genetic components in your DNA, hinting at a deep connection between your energetic and biological makeup.

SO, WHAT'S THE BIG IDEA?

At this point, you might be saying to yourself, *My spiritual practice already incorporates one or several of these ancient wisdoms; what does Human Design have to offer that I'm not already getting from my current practice?*

Or, you might be wondering, *If Human Design is a synthesis of four ancient ideas, what makes it relevant to my life right now?*

Well, get ready . . . because here's the mind-blowing part – the fifth, final and crucial component of Human Design is quantum physics.

Unlike these individual spiritual disciplines on their own, Human Design uniquely synthesises the elements of ancient wisdom with cutting-edge science. Understanding Human Design doesn't open up some vague, metaphorical connection to a higher power; it gives you the scientifically backed tools to tap into the very real energy of the Universe and its direct impact on you, your body and your life path.

Allow me to explain.

Quantum physics is a scientific field that explores the behaviour of subatomic particles, like electrons and photons. One of the fundamental principles of quantum physics is the idea of superposition. You'd need a whole book to get into the weeds on superposition, but essentially it means that subatomic particles can exist in multiple states simultaneously until they are observed or measured.

Human Design makes the case that our energetic blueprint is influenced by the movement of subatomic particles within our bodies. Quantum physics backs this up – according to the science, everything in the Universe, including our bodies, is influenced by these tiny particles called neutrinos. As these Neutrinos pass through you and the celestial bodies, they imprint you with the energies of each planet. This imprinting becomes your birth or natal chart.

You can think of the elements described in Human Design, which you'll learn all about over the course of this book, as the macro-level manifestation of the quantum activity taking place inside of us.

WHAT ARE NEUTRINOS?

Neutrinos are elusive subatomic particles. The sun produces roughly 70 per cent of all neutrinos that travel through our solar system, while the other 30 per cent of neutrinos are emitted by other stars in our galaxy and a small amount come from the planet Jupiter.

In 1991, Ra Uru Hu, the founder of Human Design, wrote that neutrinos had mass - and that as an energetic substance travelling through the universe, they have the capacity to connect human beings to the wider energy of the Universe, thereby underpinning the science behind Human Design. Mainstream science didn't catch up to the idea that neutrinos had mass until nearly 20 years after Ra's publication, when Takaaki Kajita and Arthur B. McDonald won a Nobel Prize for discovering neutrino oscillations, which shows that neutrinos do have mass.

Now let's come back to the idea of superposition in quantum physics. Superposition aligns with certain aspects of Human Design. Remember how particles can exist in multiple states at the same time? Well, so can we, energetically speaking. Human Design suggests that we are a combination of different energy types, Centres and Channels. These different aspects can come together in unique ways to create our individual Design. It's like a symphony of energies, all playing their part simultaneously. By pairing these basic facts about quantum physics with the personal truths you'll discover in your chart, you can start to accept – and even find power in – the many conflicting multitudes of energy playing out through you at all times.

And, just as observing or measuring particles collapses their wave-like behaviour into a specific state, Human Design acknowledges that our experiences and conditioning can influence the way our energetic blueprint manifests. It suggests that societal conditioning, social influences from family, friends, neighbours and colleagues and our own choices shape our energy Centres and the way we express ourselves in the world. In a way, it's like our conscious awareness collapses the probabilities and potentials of our energetic Design into a specific expression.

But – another way of being also exists.

Just because you are who the world has made you doesn't mean you were *born* to be what the world has made you, or that who you are now is all you can ever be.

What you've been conditioned to be and what you've been Designed to be are different, simultaneously existing versions of you. The great experiment of Human Design is the act of

opening the box, seeing the cat for what it really is and accepting the reality of who you were born to be over the enforced
conditioning of who you are in this incomplete moment. This
deconditioning, or 'reconditioning' as I like to call it, is the
ultimate answer to uncovering your true potential, rejecting
what you've been told and instead owning what is true for you
on a soul level, so that you can live your life to the absolute
fullest.

2.
WHAT CAN HUMAN DESIGN DO FOR ME?

Now that you understand the absolute fundamentals of Human Design and where it came from, you might be wondering: *Okay, so now what? What does this complex system with all of its esoteric and scientific elements really have to do with me, one person trying to make their way in the world? How can understanding all these lofty topics help me live a more fulfilling life now?*

The answer is a lot simpler than you might imagine: you *don't* have to understand all these lofty topics to begin experimenting with Human Design.

Instead, you must trust that you have all the answers you will ever need inside of you. Trust that this book will teach you how to access those answers so that you can step purposefully into the life you were Designed – and deserve – to live.

Human Design can help you let go of societal pressure and discover your unique shine.

Instead of trying to 'get it right' – in your Human Design journey, or in your life in general – I invite you to take Imperfect

Action towards your dreams every day. Remind yourself that you are always winning or learning – never failing.

LET'S TALK ABOUT ALIGNMENT AND AUTHENTICITY

Throughout the course of this book, I often talk about aligning, or living in/acting in/stepping into 'Alignment' with your Design.

What I mean by this is simple: Alignment is the feeling of resonance, ease and flow you'll feel when you follow the guidance of your Human Design.

That guidance depends on your unique energetic makeup, and as you work through Part 2 of this book, you'll have the chance to dive deep into what kind of guidance you're Designed to make use of when it comes to how you can make the most of your energy, set boundaries around your gifts, address your challenges, discover what feels correct for you, make decisions that serve you and more.

Note that acting in Alignment with your Design does not mean following the guidance set out in this book - or any other Human Design guidance - blindly. It's about taking the structure and details of your Design and experimenting with them, embodying and integrating them beyond the learning mind and into the physical body. So you begin to see more of what you want and less of what you don't. Taking what you discover - the new choices, behaviours and knowledge your Design provides - and allowing it to empower you to live in a way that feels correct for you, rather than acting and living at the mercy of anyone else's ideas about who and how you should be.

Another phrase I'll use a lot over the course of this book is 'authentic'.

When I talk about authenticity in the context of Human Design, I'm talking about your truest, most natural self, the person behind the conditioning and underneath the mask. The version of you that you were born - *Designed* - to be, before societal conditioning told you that success and happiness are dictated by your ability to fit in, hustle and compete.

You are extraordinary, even if your ego and inner critic tell you otherwise. You matter and this planet needs you to thrive so we can all thrive. Authenticity is all about breaking the rules you have been taught to follow and playing by your own rules.

You're specifically Designed to live in a very unique way, and when you do, then you will thrive in all areas of your life - career, relationships, well-being, money and adventure. You will know your superpowers, gifts and talents; others will love to receive all you have to give, and you will have plenty to keep for yourself.

Now is the time to stop giving your power away to others and empower yourself to live a purpose-driven life, where you feel like you matter and have an impact, a life in which *you* are the lead character of your movie and you deeply love, trust and accept *you*. A life that is fulfilling and heart-led.

I know that embracing your shine, or even figuring out how to see it, is no easy task. We live in a world that tells us who to be from the moment of conception. Once we're born, we listen, watch and learn how to receive love, who we need to be to be taken care of, what we need to do to fit in and how we need to behave to receive love. This is called conditioning.

RECONDITION YOUR MIND

Human Design offers a pathway to help you break out of your conditioning and live from authenticity instead.

'Reconditioning' is the process where you start to let go of societal pressures, expectations and influences that have shaped your behaviour and decisions (these external factors 'condition' your subconscious mind to create behaviours that are inauthentic, driven to receive love, nurturing and belonging – but creating habits that do not serve you and lead to challenging relationships and experiences.)

Reconditioning is all about getting in touch with your truest, most authentic self and making choices that align with your own inner guidance and authority, rather than following what you've been told you should do or be. It's all about finding your authentic path and living in a way that feels right for you, rather than trying to fit into someone else's mould.

When you step into your Human Design, when you accept that there is so much more at work in the world – in the Universe – that the societal rules you've been conditioned to follow and the visions of success you've been conditioned to pursue are bogus, that's when your Human Design experiment can really begin.

Helping you to recondition is the primary function of Human Design – *that's* what all of this has to do with you. Up until now, you've probably been operating as if you need to fit into the world, because you've been conditioned to see the things that make you unique as shortcomings and problems. But through reconditioning, and through embracing your unique Design, you will learn that you don't need to try to fit into the world – you're already an essential and valuable piece of it, exactly as you are.

YOUR MATTER

I like to think of planet Earth and all her life as an intricate puzzle where each piece is doing its part to contribute to the whole. Even the tiniest piece matters. It needs to show up exactly as it was designed to be or the puzzle and planet Earth will be incomplete. Each piece is unique, and each piece is equally important. You are one of these important puzzle pieces, and the only way we can unite this planet is to have every piece being uniquely itself.

You may be a small piece of the puzzle, but your potential is as infinite as the Universe, and once you embrace the guidance of your Human Design - the bigness, the unstoppable powerful force of you - you'll be free and equipped to live the life you were meant to, and to contribute more meaningfully to the world around you.

The beauty of Human Design is that it's as micro as it is macro – the Universe may be big, but because it left its imprint on you at birth it exists and works just as much *within* you as it does around you and beyond you.

GET EMPOWERED TO COCREATE WITH THE UNIVERSE

The energy that created the entire Universe is the same energy that flows in you. This means that the power you need to transform your life is the same power it took to create the Universe.

Give that a minute to land: *The power you need to transform your life is the same power it took to create the Universe.*

And that power is already within you – it was encoded into your Design before you were born.

When you embrace the elements of your Design and let it guide you towards the life you've always been aligned to live, you're taking steps towards a more harmonious and effective relationship with the Universe that made you. In effect, you are telling the Universe that you're ready to finish what it started – to follow the map it gave you towards the treasure of you and your unique and wonderful life since the moment that the very first particles of you came into being.

When it comes to recognising what Human Design can do for you, the most impactful question to ask isn't really, 'How is Human Design relevant to my life?' It's, 'How can Human Design give me the tools to cocreate with the Universe, for my own personal highest good and also for the good of the entire planet?'

You probably won't be surprised to learn that there are infinite answers to that question. Human Design can help you pursue the most fulfilling career for you, it can help you identify and live your personal values and show you how best to care for those you love. It can help you define your management style, discover how best to attract more money and success and determine how best to raise your children. Human Design can help you uncover the kind of life that makes you feel most at home, the kinds of romantic relationships and friendships you want to pursue, how best to look after your own health and so much more.

It can enable you to pinpoint your biggest fears and obstacles, as well as the superpowers that will help you overcome those challenges and turn them into your greatest gifts.

All of these little answers ladder up to something bigger: Human Design can help you live out your unique life purpose *on* purpose.

LIVE *WITH* PURPOSE *ON* PURPOSE

The key to using Human Design to unlock your purpose is to first recognise that your purpose has always been a part of you, since day one. You just have to 'Know thyself', as philosopher Socrates famously said, and start working with what is already within you, instead of looking to the rest of the world to tell you who you are and what works best for you.

Because we're conditioned to believe we have to go out and succeed in all areas of our lives rather than stand in the power we already have, we often go *searching* for our purpose. We ask other people to tell us what it is. We go to the careers advisor, we go to our spiritual leaders, we go to our mentors.

But the truth is that your purpose doesn't come from what other people tell you you are. It comes from what is already within you, waiting to be activated and turned to full volume the second you start making aligned decisions.

Human Design gives you the knowledge you need to allow yourself to be guided by your own intrinsic internal wisdom – your Design shows you the map to living out what you were born to be and do. Think of your Human Design as a pair of glasses you never knew you needed; your Design is the lens you need to look through in order to clarify your purpose. It may take some time to adjust to the view, but I promise, once you've wrapped your head around what you're looking at, you won't just have a clearer idea of where you are, you'll be better able to visualise where you're going. The more you look at yourself and your world through the lens of your unique Design, the more you'll understand your unique life purpose and how you're designed to thrive.

The deeper you commit to discovering and experimenting with your Human Design, you'll not only see your purpose more clearly, you'll decode a detailed map for how to get there. And you'll realise that the destination was never some external vision of success – you were always Designed to thrive through knowing and honouring your soul. Your Human Design is the road map to discovering, and activating, your soul's unique offering to this world.

As you move through this book, you'll deepen your knowledge of how Human Design works, and you'll build a working relationship with your unique Human Design chart. Through your Human Design journey, the secrets of moving through this world *on* purpose and *with* purpose will begin to become clear. And over time, as long as you continue to commit to your personal experiment with Human Design, then acting in Alignment with your Design and, in effect, your purpose, will become instinct.

3.
READING YOUR CHART

Your Human Design is your energetic blueprint, a road map to your soul and the key to your life's purpose. It encompasses everything within you – from the very smallest subatomic particle of your body to the energetic aura that stretches beyond you and interacts with the world around you – and everything you can be.

You can access all of this knowledge, and begin the journey to understanding what it means and how you can take action on it, via your Human Design chart.

WHAT IS A HUMAN DESIGN CHART?

Like an astrological chart, your Human Design chart is generated based on the time and place of your birth, but it does *so much more* than give you a picture of what the sky looked like the night you were born and how that impacts your experiences and personality.

Instead, your Human Design chart gives you a crystal-clear picture of your unique Human Design, which includes your astrological Alignment, and also offers insight into your energetic aura and type, the energy at play in your physical, emotional and spiritual body (how best to move your body, process emotions and access your superpowers, for example), your communication style and so much more.

Over the following pages, I'm going to break down all of the components of a Human Design chart so that you can orient yourself when you look at your own. We'll cover:

- How to get your chart, and what to do with it once you have it.
- The nine key elements of your Design.
- Where to find each element on your chart.
- What areas of your life each element of your Design can help you in.
- Where to find more information about each element, within this book and beyond.

HOW CAN I GET MY CHART?

There are many free platforms online that you can use to generate your Human Design chart. All charts are generally the same, but the layout, language and colour scheme can vary from platform to platform.

For the purposes of keeping your journey through this book as simple and straightforward as possible, I recommend you generate your chart via my website, so we're always on exactly the same page when it comes to the language and layout of your chart.

You'll need:

- The date, time and location of your birth.
- A device where you can save your chart and/or a printer – keep in mind that you'll want to reference your chart regularly as you move through this book.

YOUR CHART IS WAITING FOR YOU

Generate your Human Design chart now:

Go to **www.emmadunwoody.com** to download your chart

WHAT IF I DON'T KNOW MY BIRTH TIME?

To generate an accurate Human Design chart, you do need to know the time and location of your birth. Since your chart is a map of the blueprint the Universe left on you at the moment you came into this world, the details of that moment are critical.

If you don't know your birth time, try to get your hands on your full birth certificate - it's empowering to have a copy of this for its own sake, anyway! If, for whatever reason, your birth time is not listed on your birth certificate, you can contact the hospital where you were born and ask for your birth record, or you can ask a parent or other family member who was present (though the time may not be perfectly accurate, and this may affect the effectiveness of your chart).

You can also estimate your birth time based on whatever knowledge is available to you, or even seek out astrologers who specialise in birth time rectification by cross-referencing major events in your life with astrological events that took place at the same time. Both of these options are last-case scenarios, as they likely won't result in a 100 per cent accurate answer, but they can still provide you with useful information.

If you're absolutely unable to recover your birth time, you can enter multiple times throughout the day and make note of any major changes in your Type, Authority, Profile and Strategy then use the information in this book to see what resonates most with you, and what feels true. You may not be able to get 100 per cent accuracy, but you can absolutely still play along with your Design by using your intuition and experience.

My Human Design chart immediately showed me areas in which I am fighting myself and offered practical guidance to stop. I am a rather unusual type and have been trying to fit in to conventional patterns that work for a lot of people, including family members. But this has really burned me out.

Human Design is showing me there is a way better to flow through my day and appreciate the range of humanity in other people and myself. I was never interested in astrology before this, and honestly that aspect is still a non-starter for me, but my chart is so compelling and 'just gets me' that I don't care. I'm learning all the things and loving it!

- Bernie

WHAT INFORMATION WILL I FIND IN MY CHART?

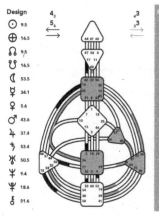 

Name	Emma Dunwoody
Type	Manifesting Generator
Strategy	To Respond
Inner Authority	Emotional – Solar Plexus
Definition	Split Definition
Profile	3 / 5
Incarnation Cross	Right Angle Cross of Planning (37/40 | 9/16)
Signature	Satisfaction
Not-Self Theme	Frustration
Digestion	Calm
Sense	Meditation
Design Sense	Outer Vision
Motivation	Desire
Perspective	Power
Environment	Valleys

When you generate your chart, you'll see it's divided into two halves.

On the left, you'll see an image that looks like a matrix of shapes (these are your Centres) connected by a series of lines. This image is called your bodygraph; it's a visual representation of how energy manifests and flows through your body, according to your unique Design.

On the right side of your chart, you'll see lines of text. This text is an interpretation of all the rich visual information you see on the left side. The text will tell you in plain terms, based on what's in your bodygraph, the key things you need to know for your Human Design experiment.

YOUR UNIQUE CHART

There are over 2 billion possible combinations of the elements on your chart. Just imagine everything that had to happen to bring your Design and *you* together exactly as you are!

I like to think this figure simultaneously highlights just how unique we all are, and reminds us that none of us are really alone either. With 8 billion people on the planet, it might be comforting to know that somewhere out there, someone else is Designed to see life the same way you do.

In this book, we'll focus on four key elements:

- Type
- Strategy
- Authority
- Profile

Mastering these four elements serves as the foundation of your Human Design journey.

Let's break them down:

TYPE

Your Human Design Type gives you the most basic information about how you're Designed and how you interact energetically with the world.

There are Five Human Design Types:

1. **Manifestors** are led by a creative urge to initiate and to inspire action in others.

2. **Generators** build great things when they are lit up and excited by the work they love.

3. **Manifesting Generators** are superhuman examples of human potential.

4. **Projectors** see deeply into the other and guide greater efficiencies.

5. **Reflectors** reflect back the truth of people and groups.

Your Type is a crucial tool for understanding how you can move through the world in a way that is authentic and supportive for you, but you are not bound to anything because of your Type.

Type is an incredibly useful method for understanding the core components of your Design and unlocking what makes you you. But think of it like a tool, not a directive. Type is not the be-all and end-all, or a prescription for who you are or who you have to be; it is a powerful jumping-off point that can give you essential insight into how you can show up in the world as your truest, most empowered self.

We'll dive more deeply into unpacking your Type and how it can help you in living a more authentic life in Part 2. Within the Type section of Part 2, we'll also cover your Strategy, as well as your Signature and Not-Self Themes.

STRATEGY

Your Strategy tells you how you're Designed to interact with the world.

Your Strategy is determined by your Type; these two elements of your chart are inexorably linked because, together, Type and Strategy define the way we can consciously let go of our conditioning and know our own, authentic truth.

Here's a basic summary of each Strategy:

Manifestors initiate and inform. You allow your flow of creativity to guide you to something new and make it come to life. It may not feel natural to inform others of what you are doing, but remember that it is not asking for permission, it's stating an intention and clearing the way for creativity to flow. Think of it as declaring the direction of your energy.

Generators respond to something external, like people, opportunities, synchronicities and signs. Write down your internal thoughts and guidance and hold it in your awareness until the Universe brings you something to respond to.

Manifesting Generators respond and inform. You are a hybrid of the Manifestor and the Generator. Being Generator first and foremost, you are here to respond to your external environment, so wait for the Universe to send something to respond to. Once you have your external something to respond to, inform others as you spring into action. Remember, you're not asking for permission, just letting others know what your huge energy is off to create.

Projectors wait for the invitation. You need to wait to be recognised for your amazing wisdom or to share the potential you see in others before offering your guidance. If you jump the gun and offer guidance without being invited, it will likely be met with resistance and not received well.

Reflectors wait 28 days or a lunar cycle. As the moon moves through your Design every 28 days, you sample how decisions, people or places make you feel, and with time you will feel into what is correct and not correct for you. Don't rush, in time you will know what's aligned for you.

You'll have the opportunity to explore and experiment with your Strategy in more depth in the Type and Strategy chapter (page 69) in Part 2 of this book.

AUTHORITY

Your Authority provides guidance for decision-making based on your unique Design and your consistent energetic superpowers. Understanding your Authority will empower you to make choices that align with your most authentic self.

Unlike Strategy, your Authority is not always aligned to Type. Generators, Manifestors, Projectors, Reflectors and Manifesting Generators can all have an Emotional Authority, for example.

There are seven Authorities in Human Design:

1. **Emotional Authority:** You are most aligned to your Design when you give yourself time to gain emotional clarity when making decisions.

2. **Sacral Authority:** You need to listen to your body's natural, physical gut instinct for what is and isn't correct for you in every moment.

3. **Splenic Authority:** Your Authority manifests as a subtle, intuitive sense of knowing that shows up in the moment.

4. **Ego Authority:** Your most authentic decisions come from talking out, recognising and acting on what your heart desires.

5. **Self-Directed Authority:** You're Designed to move towards a sense of love in all of your decisions. It helps you

to talk out your options and bounce off another person so you can hear which direction will lead you towards more love.

6. **Mental Projector Authority:** Your Authority manifests when you get your mind out of the way and listen to your own voice as you process decisions.

7. **No Inner Authority:** This rare Authority, which may also be referred to Lunar Authority, only shows up in Reflector types. You are designed to sample life; decisions are made by giving yourself time to get to know how opportunities, people and places make you feel before settling on a decision. The 28-day lunar cycle is the ideal time to wait to make big decisions.

When you're ready to dive more deeply into your Authority, and how you can lean on it to help you make decisions that are aligned with your Design, head over to page 133.

PROFILE

Your Profile identifies significant themes that play out in every area of your life. Profile is how we move through the world, described by Ra Uru Hu as the costume of our purpose. Every Profile is made up of a combination of two 'Lines' that make up your Personality, or your conscious experience, and your Design, or your unconscious experience.

Let's break down the six Lines that combine to create your Profile:

Line 1: People with Line 1 in their Profile are natural learners and authorities. You activate your purpose through seeking out and sharing knowledge.

Line 2: People with Line 2 in their Profile are born talents; you are here to share your natural gifts. You activate your purpose when you honour your natural talents.

Line 3: People with Line 3 in their Profile are Designed to learn by experimentation through trial and error. You activate your purpose when you break away from convention and experiment.

Line 4: People with Line 4 in their Profile thrive in community and relationships. You activate your purpose when you're connected to and supported by other people who share your values.

Line 5: People with Line 5 in their Profile are here to heal, solve and lead. You activate your purpose when you focus on healing yourself and use your experience to help others heal.

Line 6: People with Line 6 in their profile grow into great sources of wisdom over time. You activate your purpose when you cultivate patience and allow yourself the time you need to learn and reflect before you share your wisdom.

In Part 3, I'll guide you through the Profile Lines in depth and help you understand how to recognise and work with your Personality and Design lines (page 217).

Now that you have a basic working knowledge of these four key components in your bodygraph (Type, Strategy, Authority, and Profile) your Human Design experiment has officially begun.

CENTRES

To navigate your chart with confidence, and better understand the underpinning philosophy that guides the foundational

Visual Representation of the Centres

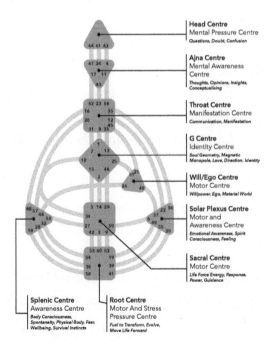

Head Centre
Mental Pressure Centre
Questions, Doubt, Confusion

Ajna Centre
Mental Awareness Centre
Thoughts, Opinions, Insights, Conceptualising

Throat Centre
Manifestation Centre
Communication, Manifestation

G Centre
Identity Centre
Soul Geometry, Magnetic Monopole, Love, Direction, Identity

Will/Ego Centre
Motor Centre
Willpower, Ego, Material World

Solar Plexus Centre
Motor and Awareness Centre
Emotional Awareness, Spirit Consciousness, Feeling

Sacral Centre
Motor Centre
Life Force Energy, Response, Power, Guidance

Splenic Centre
Awareness Centre
Body Consciousness, Spontaneity, Physical Body, Fear, Wellbeing, Survival Instincts

Root Centre
Motor And Stress Pressure Centre
Fuel to Transform, Evolve, Move Life Forward

elements of your Design, you'll also want to get familiar with one key element of your bodygraph: your Centres.

CENTRES AND CHAKRAS

The Human Design Centres are rooted in the Buddhist and Hindu Chakra system. If you're interested in learning more about how these traditions intersect and overlap in the context of Human Design, check out this episode of The Human Design Podcast:

www.emmadunwoody.com/blog/the-human-design-podcast-episode-266-the-human-design-roadmap-part-7-centres-definition-made-simple

---

The energy Centres of the body influence how we interact with the world and others. Each Centre is associated with a different Chakra in the body, and the energy that part of the body sources (your Head Centre sources your mental processing, while your Throat Centre sources the energy that flows through you when you communicate). There are nine Centres in Human Design:

1. **Head Centre:** The Head Centre is the source of inspiration and ideas, influencing our mental processes.

2. **Ajna Centre:** The Ajna Centre is responsible for conceptualisation and understanding, shaping our thought patterns.

3.   **Throat Centre:** The Throat Centre governs
     communication and manifestation, influencing how we
     express ourselves in the world.

4.   **G Centre:** The G Centre, sometimes known as the Identity
     Centre, shapes our sense of self-direction and love.

5.   **Will Centre:** The Will Centre, also known as the Heart or
     Ego Centre, governs willpower and ego, influencing our
     drive and sense of self-worth.

6.   **Solar Plexus Centre:** The Solar Plexus Centre governs
     emotions and feelings, shaping our emotional responses to
     the world.

7.   **Sacral Centre:** The Sacral Centre is the seat of life force
     and vitality, influencing our ability to respond and
     generate energy.

8.   **Splenic Centre:** The Splenic Centre governs survival,
     well-being, intuition and instinct, influencing our
     awareness of potential threats and opportunities.

9.   **Root Centre:** The Root Centre governs the fuel to
     progress, stress and pressure, shaping your motivation to
     get things done or not.

The Centres fall into three categories, with some Centres falling into multiple:

1. **Awareness Centres:** Ajna, Splenic, Solar Plexus. These Centres generate awareness in the body, mental awareness, physical awareness and emotional awareness.

2. **Motor Centres:** Sacral, Root, Solar Plexus, Will (also known as Heart and Ego). These Centres generate action or motorised energy – the energy to work, the fuel to get things done, express emotion and willpower.

3. **Pressure Centres:** Ajna, Root. These Centres apply pressure to think and work things out and to progress and get things done.

In your chart, certain Centres will be defined or undefined. You'll recognise which Centres are defined in your chart based on which ones are coloured in. If a Centre is coloured in, that means it's defined, and if a Centre is not coloured in, that means it's not defined for you. When a Centre is defined, that means that you have a consistent source of energy flowing from this Centre, and that you have unique gifts based on where that energy comes from. When a Centre is undefined in you, that means that the energy that flows through that Centre is not sourced from within you, but is influenced based on your environment and the people you're surrounded by.

Each chart/bodygraph will have different configurations of defined and undefined Centres. Know that this is perfect, because you are perfect exactly as you are Designed. All Centres have pros and cons in their definition or openness (undefined). Whether a Centre is defined or undefined can have profound implications for your experiences, shaping everything from your communication styles to your sense of identity.

DIVE DEEPER INTO DEFINITION

In Part 2, you'll learn about your Authority, which is determined by which Centres are defined for you. But there's even more to learn about how your defined and undefined Centres play out in your Design. When you feel comfortable with the material in this book and are ready to experiment further with your Definition, check out this episode from The Human Design Podcast:

www.emmadunwoody.com/blog/the-human-design-podcast-episode-266-the-human-design-roadmap-part-7-centres-definition-made-simple

4.
HUMAN DESIGN SUCCESS STORIES

Human Design gives you the tools to know and live your greatest potential. There's so much power in knowing what's possible, not just based on what your chart shows you, but also in seeing how other people have successfully embraced their Design so they can live out their dreams.

Since beginning my own Human Design experiment, I've helped thousands of people uncover and act in Alignment with their Designs through retreats, workshops, my membership and mastermind communities and one-to-one coaching. I've spoken to and heard from thousands more through my show, The Human Design Podcast, about how Human Design is helping people transform their lives.

I want to tell you about a few of my favourite stories of transformation through Human Design now, so that you can begin to envision what's possible for you. But before I share these stories, remember – your journey is unique, and so is your version of success when you live authentically in line with who you are. These stories are windows into what's possible, not rubrics to condition you into chasing any one idea of success.

THE PURPOSE-DRIVEN CEO

Heather was a senior manager driven to live out her purpose to lead. She was a long-standing coaching client of mine, and one of the first business leaders I introduced to Human Design.

Heather had always been one of those dream clients to work with – willing, open, curious, powerful and deeply driven to lead purposefully. She was already thriving at work; she was already a really good manager. By all accounts, she was smashing it. And she felt called to more.

In a session several years ago, she shared a goal with me. The confession was barely a whisper; I had to ask her to repeat herself.

'Speak up,' I told her. 'If you want it, own it.'

She took a big breath, and this time I heard her loud and clear:

'I want to be a CEO within the next eight years.'

'Brilliant,' I said. 'Let's do it!'

Then I took a deep breath of my own and a big risk:

'I know it sounds woo-woo, but what if I told you that telling me your birth time could help us make this happen for you faster?'

Just three years later, she and I were cheering over lunch to her first CEO role.

Committing to her Human Design experiment was a critical part of Heather's rocket to success. Once we unpacked her chart, all kinds of opportunities to work smarter, not harder, started to emerge. She found courage to say 'no', put boundaries in place and was able to truly put her clients first for better outcomes all around.

By diving deep into her Manifesting Generator type, we were able to reallocate her energy at work. Before, she had spent a lot of time trying to be perfect, finish everything and learn everything in detail, when what she needed was space to be guided by her multipassionate energy, to jump in and learn what she needed and then get out before completing, to focus on a number of projects at a high level, instead of getting stuck in the weeds on every single thing she oversaw as a manager. She empowered her team, demonstrated what was possible and threw out what was no longer working, replacing it with upgraded solutions.

As a Line 5 (more on this on page 245), she had a talent for solving problems, but this led to a belief that she had to solve everyone's problems on her own, and often left her with little time to focus on her own development. Naming this challenge was the first step in helping her set clear boundaries and recognise the importance of empowering delegation in her work.

While she was learning to delegate, she was also experimenting with her Sacral Authority by trusting her gut instead of overthinking every decision she made at work. Today, she's celebrated as a leader with incredible instincts.

When Heather started living in Alignment with who she really is, the results for her career were undeniable. She trusted her own internal guidance system. She relied on the knowledge her chart offered about how she was Designed to lead. And she didn't stop there – she continued to return to her Design, not just to help her make decisions at work, but to guide all aspects of her life.

THE DESIGN-LED PARENT

Valerie spent her entire life being the person who people ran to for an open ear, support and help. She saw herself as a doer, a fixer, a problem solver and her sense of worth was entirely bound up in what she had to offer other people in her life. She felt she had to earn love through being useful. As a result, she struggled to set boundaries, and her own needs and desires remained unconscious as she put all of her energy into being who other people needed her to be.

Becoming a parent amplified her view of herself as someone who needed to be what others – her children specifically – needed. For years as her family grew, Valerie kept herself busy ensuring everyone was taken care of physically, emotionally and more before taking care of herself. On the surface it worked: she and her family had a beautiful life. But she was slowly running herself ragged, ignoring her own phys-ical and mental health in order to prioritise the other people in her life. She told herself, 'When everyone else is good, *then* I can work on myself and follow my dreams.'

As her children got older, Valerie noticed they didn't seem happy, despite all of the doing and fixing she did for them. And the truth was, she wasn't happy either. So she chose to look inward, and found Human Design along her journey. Human Design gave her a language that she connected with on a cellular level. And through running her experiment, she recognised shifts in herself and in her whole family.

Learning about her Human Design Type and Profile helped Valerie realise and own the fact that, despite her conditioning, she's not here to 'do' everything for everyone. Instead, as a Projector, she is here to be a guide.

Human Design helped her embrace a newfound peace, presence and happiness in her role as a mother. Long gone are the days of running around, fixing and doing everything for everyone. She's able to be present for her children without trying to fix or control everything, and the communication in her household has improved.

She recently told me:

'What I love most is my ability to understand my children's Human Design chart and guide and encourage who they are – not who I *think* they should be. To help them stay connected to their inner truth and light. We are not running around from activity to activity. Instead we intentionally commit to schools, friendships and activities that feel correct for us and light us up. And it's a beautiful journey that also changes as we change in life. I wouldn't have it any other way and I see this as the future for all families!'

THE SLEEPER COACH

When I first started working with Bronwyn on unpacking and embracing her Design, she was a teacher. Her job felt purposeful enough; she knew she loved working with kids to help them thrive, and that made her days feel meaningful. But she also knew something wasn't right. She was tired and run-down all the time, and even though she loved her students, she didn't feel like she was able to sustain the energy they required from her, or that her work was as rewarding as the effort she was putting in. She was stifled by rigid curriculum requirements and knew she wasn't making the kind of impact she was capable of. She had already tried a number of different roles within the school, but nothing felt like the right fit.

Because she was tired all the time, she didn't feel like she had the energy to show up enough for her students, or her own children, in a fulfilling, energising way.

Through coming to understand her Design, Bronwyn realised her primary motivation for becoming a teacher was bound up in her conditioned belief that she needed to have a 'safe and consistent' career, the 'American Dream' life.

But in trying to do the thing she'd been conditioned to do by her family and the education path she'd taken, she was wearing herself out doing work that didn't take her own needs, talents and energy into account. She felt undervalued and unseen by those closest to her.

As a Projector, she just wasn't Designed to stand in a classroom with all of these little sacral beings whose energy she was amplifying and reflecting back. It simply wasn't an environment that made the most of who she is at her core.

While this discovery led to a painful yet liberating decision to leave her career behind, it didn't end in abandoning teaching altogether.

Today, Bronwyn teaches on her own terms, as a Human Design coach and trainer on my team. The flexibility, reduced hours and authoritorial nature of her work as a coach are much better suited to her natural energy. She's no longer beholden to some institution's curriculum, to hours that don't suit her life or to physically demanding work conditions that wear her out.

And as far as that need to have an acceptable career goes, she's making more money than she ever did at primary school, on her own terms, through the power of her Design.

5.
RUNNING YOUR EXPERIMENT

Okay, beautiful human, you're almost ready to leap headfirst into discovering the magic of your unique Design. But before we dive deep into the guidance Human Design has to offer you based on your Human Design Type, Strategy, Authority and Profile, there's one more important thing I want to equip you with before we begin: my tried-and-tested method for learning and working with your unique Design in a sustainable and transformational way.

By now you'll have noticed how often I refer to your Human Design journey as an experiment. As an expert in behavioural science, I take that language very seriously, and I mean it when I say that your experience with Human Design is meant to be full of trials, errors and beautiful discoveries that lead you ever closer to the truths that will set you free to be who you are. Your Human Design is not a rule book for you to follow to the letter; it's an experimentation model that will help you make new discoveries about yourself that empower you to live a more fulfilled, authentic life.

Taking on a mindset of experimentation and discovery is absolutely crucial if you want to go beyond knowing the facts of your Design so that you can allow them to transform your life into the beautiful experience you were meant to live.

It's vital to recognise that your Human Design can't do anything for you if you aren't willing to experiment with the information your Design offers to you.

When you free yourself to run your Human Design experiment, rather than to merely follow the facts of your Design blindly, that's when the magic is really going to happen. Experimenting with your Design will empower you to find new connections between the unique elements of your chart, discover new ways of working that suit your unique energetic makeup and get clear on the kinds of people and environments that bring out the most authentic, fulfilled version of you.

So what does running your Human Design experiment actually look like? Let me break down the model I use when working with clients, which is rooted in research-backed behavioural science.

I recommend working through this model for every element of your Human Design chart, starting with the elements we'll cover in depth in this book – your Type and Strategy, your Authority and your Profile.

MY SIX-STEP TRANSFORMATION HUMAN DESIGN EXPERIMENT MODEL

1. Learn.

2. Take Imperfect Action.

3. Record your results.

4. Test what works.

5. Let go of what doesn't work for you.

6. Repeat.

LEARN

The first step in your experiment is to achieve or experience.

Start by setting an intention around what you want to learn about. You might say, 'My intention is to discover how my Strategy guides me to more aligned choices, decisions and opportunities.'

Then, dive into your research. Depending on what feels correct for you, your research might be a combination of:

*   Reading the sections of this book that are relevant to topics you want to learn about.

- Listening to episodes of my podcast that dive deep into what you want to learn.
- Speaking to people in your life who have knowledge about the topic you want to learn about.
- Seeking out community around the topic you want to learn about (I run a beautiful community that you can find out more about on my website).

In the learning phase, focus on finding the correct knowledge for you. This is a hugely important step, but remember it's only the beginning, so don't get stuck in an endless loop studying. Think of this phase like learning the language of your topic, so that later on you have the vocabulary you need to write poetry.

The next two phases of the experiment model are extensions of the learning process, so trust that even though you don't have all the detailed answers when you move forward, you'll continue to learn and get closer to those details as you move through the experiment model.

Use your journal (or other record-keeping method, like voice notes, a notes app or a video diary) to make notes about what you learn, ask yourself questions about what you still want to discover, and keep track of your progress as you learn.

TAKE IMPERFECT ACTION

Once you've devoted some energy to learning, it's time to take Imperfect Action.

Taking Imperfect Action means practising what you're learning. It's about giving yourself permission to act, without pressuring yourself to get it right on the first – or even the fiftieth – try. Taking Imperfect Action is the bedrock of my approach to Human Design, and the key to overcoming your societal conditioning, uncovering your most authentic self and ultimately transforming your life with the help of your Human Design.

Taking Imperfect Action is as simple as it is hard – all you have to do is try taking action based on what you've learned.

Throughout this book, I offer mini Human Design experiment exercises to help you take Imperfect Action based on the subject material in the section you're reading.

It's important you understand that this will be messy and imperfect in the beginning and that your only job is to practise what you're learning. Remember, in Human Design you are always *winning* or *learning* – there is no such thing as failure.

Use your journal (or other record-keeping method) to set intentions about the Imperfect Action you plan to take, and to hold yourself accountable to those plans.

RECORD YOUR RESULTS

Put simply, you need to commit the results of your Imperfect Action to paper, voice note or video. Recording results is a very important part of changing your brain, behaviour and life. This is because to change your life, you must change your identity. To do that, the brain needs evidence that it's safe to change – the record of your results is that evidence.

Use your journal (or other record-keeping method) to record the results of your Imperfect Actions. Reflect back on what you've already recorded about what you learned and the action you intended to take, then record the outcome:

- What happened when you experimented with a specific part of your Design?
- How did you feel in your body?
- What did you learn? How did it make your life specifically better?

TEST WHAT WORKS

One you've recorded and reflected on your results, it's time to test what works. In any experiment, we know something 'works' when it's repeatable – this is where the next step of your Human Design experiment comes in.

You'll need to commit to continue taking the actions that work, repeating and refining what works as you do. Through this process, you'll move from unconscious incompetence (where you were before learning about Human Design and the specific topic you're experimenting with) to conscious incompetence (conscious of what you don't know – probably where you're at now), then conscious competence (consciously building experience and getting the hang of it) and finally to unconscious competence (mastery, unconscious habit).

During the 'Test what works' phase, take time to:

- Review your notes and journal to see what the patterns are – what has been working, and what do you need to let go of or stop doing?
- Get clear on how it feels in your body when you're taking these actions and getting aligned.
- Review how life is specifically better based on the actions you've taken and the results you've achieved.
- Keep experimenting and implementing what's working.

Avoid comparing your experiment to anyone else's at this stage or ever; everyone is different, and so is everyone's journey with their Design. Trust your experiment and ultimately your results. Ask yourself, *Am I getting the results I want?* If 'yes', then great, keep going. If 'no', then return to the 'Take Imperfect Action' phase and keep experimenting until your results feel correct for you.

Use your journal (or other record-keeping method) as a guide you can refer back to, and as a place to reflect and review on what's working and to record the ongoing results of your tests.

LET GO OF WHAT DOESN'T WORK FOR YOU

As you identify what delivers the results you want, let go of what doesn't work for you.

Seeing Human Design as an experiment means accepting that the journey is unique to everyone. There will be some knowledge that resonates and some that doesn't, and that's okay! At this point in your experiment, it's time to let go of what is not working.

Let go of:

- What your mind is telling you that you 'should do' to succeed in your experiment. Focus on what feels good in your body instead.
- Anything that feels forced.
- Comparing yourself to anyone else – this is your Design and your unique experience.
- Anything that doesn't feel true for you.

Use your journal (or other record-keeping method) as a guide you can refer back to. Use your reflections on what you learn, what actions you take, what results you see and how you feel about all of it to identify what's not working for you. Then record your intentions to let go of those things, and record how you're going to continue in the direction of what does work for you.

REPEAT

Continue to repeat the experimentation process throughout your Human Design journey. Use this model to experiment with every element of your Human Design, starting with each element in this book: your Type and Strategy, your

Authority and your Profile. Remember that your experiment is never-ending, and that's a good thing. Your chart is packed with elements you can continue to experiment with as you gain more confidence on your Human Design journey, and there will always be new opportunities to experiment with the elements you'll get to know over the course of this book.

For example, in your first reading of this book, you may be specifically interested in experimenting with how your Strategy and Authority can help you thrive in your career or relationship. You may return to these foundational elements later to experiment with how your Strategy and Authority can help you show up as a parent, how to action a creative project or how to navigate retirement. There's no shortage of experiments to run – and that's the beauty of Human Design. The wealth of knowledge it has to offer you about yourself can be applied in so many different contexts, and you'll be able to keep working and experimenting with your Design in new ways over the course of your whole life.

TRY THIS

Pull out your own chart and take note of your Type, Strategy and Authority. Journal or meditate on the following questions:

- Which resonates most deeply with me – my Type, my Strategy or my Authority?

- What questions do I still have about my Type, Strategy and/ or Authority?

- How can I experiment with what I have learned about my Strategy and my Authority?

- What three specific things can I do right away?

Experimenting with my Human Design has changed everything!

I am three years into my journey now, and I am a completely different person. I have played and experimented with *exactly* how the universe brings me external clues and how my Emotional Authority feels within me. My life has become quite magical!

I no longer worry about pro-and-con lists. Human Design has taught me how to dance with the Universe and give importance to the signs that I never knew were all around me. It's helped me get into my body, and out of my head. My life has quite literally done a magical 180° since diving into Human Design. I am empowered as I transition into exactly who my soul wants me to be in this lifetime, and even when there are hard times, the signs and clarity are still there. When we don't pay attention to signs and our Authority, it is like saying to our higher power that we know better. I'm done with 'knowing better'. I choose to dance in the magic instead.

– Tiffany

KEEP IT SIMPLE

In the earliest days of running your Human Design experiment, focus on a commitment to learning about and experimenting with two key elements of your chart: your Strategy and your Authority.

Remember, your Strategy is linked to your Human Design Type and guides you towards how you're Designed to interact with the world. Meanwhile, your Authority is your internal guidance system; it tells you how you best make decisions that are correct for you, according to your unique Design.

Strategy and Authority are the only elements you need to begin to unlock and experiment with your Design. As soon as you start to tune into the wisdom of your Strategy and Authority, you won't just feel more satisfied, confident and happy, you're also guaranteed to be more effective for your community – and by that I mean not just the people you interact with on a daily basis, but also the world at large.

Getting a handle on these two elements of your chart provides the guardrails for how you will activate all the other knowledge contained in this book, so take some time to really dive into how you relate to your Strategy and Authority, and consider what questions you have about them.

Your Strategy and Authority won't tell you who to be – only you can unlock the secrets to expressing the unique energies within you. Any of the five Human Design Types may feel called to parenthood, creative arts, business, tech innovation – the list goes on, because no matter your Design, every door is open to you. What your Strategy and Authority *can* tell you is how you can align your energy and your decisions with who you already are at your core and what your heart and soul really desire. These are tools made to help you reveal yourself to you, to help you stand in your truth and your power, not prescriptions for who you have to be or how you have to act.

ALWAYS BRING IT BACK TO BASICS

Whenever my friends and clients come to me agonising over a detail in their chart that they just can't make sense of, or trying to solve a tricky problem in their lives that they just can't seem to navigate, the first thing I do is invite them to return to their Strategy and Authority.

And when I'm navigating my own challenges or making big decisions, I do the same thing: align with my Strategy and Authority, and trust that if I don't know right now, the answers and clarity will come in divine timing.

These days, I also take time to reflect on my whole chart and pay attention to what's jumping out at me. Or I explore what's coming up as a hot topic in my community and focus on that. I trust that whatever I'm seeing 'out there' is something I must look at 'in here' – in me.

But I need you to know that even after more than two decades of personal, professional and spiritual growth and six years of my own Human Design experiment and coaching others, I always bring it back to basics first. Because if I'm out of

Alignment with my Strategy or Authority, there's really no point looking any further until I've got that sorted.

All of that's to say that you can start mastering these basic building blocks of Human Design right now, and trust that these two elements of your chart are tools you can turn to every minute of every day, even if you never memorise or fully understand every detail of your chart.

I strongly recommend that you do continue on your journey to unpack your chart beyond your Strategy and Authority – because if two elements can be so game-changing, imagine what you can do with the full arsenal of self-knowledge that your Design provides.

Armed with your Strategy and Authority, you are ready to begin your Human Design experiment today. Don't let overwhelm, fear or impostor syndrome scare you – because by the time you're done with this book, you'll have learned a universe of ways to understand and cope with those scary feelings.

Your Design is a permission slip to be you, and this book is a permission slip to find your own strength through experimenting with your Design. And this moment is your permission slip to stop waiting around and embrace your Design right now. No more waiting. No more gatekeeping. No more gurus. Just incredible, capable, beautifully Designed you.

Start with these basics today and then trust this book – and yourself – to be your guide as you go deeper.

PART 2

YOUR DESIGN MADE SIMPLE

6.
YOUR TYPE AND STRATEGY

Your Type and Strategy form the basis of your Human Design chart. It doesn't get more simple or more direct than these two elements, and gaining a firm understanding of them is the key to unlocking the rest of your Human Design experiment.

To begin, let's talk about Type. Your Type is a crucial tool for understanding how you can move through the world in a way that is authentic and supportive for you.

There are five types: Manifestor, Generator, Manifesting Generator, Projector and Reflector, and everyone who's ever been born falls into one of these Types, based on the unique makeup of their Human Design bodygraph.

Before you skip straight to the pages that cover your Type, allow me to let you in on a little secret: Type is overhyped in the Human Design world.

The truth is that when Ra Uru Hu first channelled the 'Voice' that unveiled the mysteries of Human Design, Types weren't part of the initial vocabulary. They were conceived later, as a kind of shorthand for grouping different energy patterns together – an early attempt to make Human Design more accessible. And it worked – being able to quickly understand this basic building block of your chart is essential, especially when you're first starting to experiment with your Design. However, don't fall into the trap of defining yourself solely by your Type.

TO UNDERSTAND YOUR TYPE, REVIEW YOUR CENTRES

Back on page 41, I walked you through the basics of the Human Design Centres. If you skimmed that part, I encourage you to go back and give it a closer study, because it offers foundational knowledge that will help you as you uncover your Type.

The Centres that are defined or undefined for you will dictate your Type, so to really live your authentic self, your purpose and your Design, you must get to know your Centres - they have so much rich value to offer, including showing where you are most susceptible to conditioning and how you influence and express your energy.

Type is incredibly useful for understanding the core components of your Design and unlocking what makes you you. Think of it like a container, or like scaffolding. It gives you structure, but it doesn't define the contents. Your container gets filled with all the other nuances and details of your chart, and how *you* bring that uniqueness to life. So even if you have the same Type or 'container' as someone else, what that container is filled with will be completely different from the next person.

Put simply: Type is not the be-all and end-all, or a prescription for who you are or who you have to be, but it *is* a powerful jumping-off point that can give you essential insight into your energy.

DISCOVER YOUR TYPE

Pull up your Human Design bodygraph. (If you don't have one yet, you can get yours at emmadunwoody.com now.)

Underneath the full-colour bodygraph image, you'll see your name, and directly beneath that, you'll see your Human Design Type.

Once you've finished reading this introduction to Type and Strategy, go through the chapter until you find the section on your Type. Give it a read, and make notes on what resonates with you, what surprises you and what you resist or don't like when it comes to your Type.

YOUR TYPE DICTATES YOUR STRATEGY

Each Type corresponds to a specific Strategy, the method by which you can act in Alignment with your Design. Manifestors are Designed to Initiate and Inform; Generators are Designed to Respond; Manifesting Generators are Designed to Respond and Inform; Projectors are Designed to Wait for an Invitation; and Reflectors are Designed to Follow the 28-day Moon Cycle.

There are two primary categories for Strategy – to 'Initiate' and to 'Respond'. Manifestors Initiate – their Strategy comes from an internal urge or inspiration; this Type initiates things. Meanwhile, the remaining four types Respond; each type has their own way of responding authentically.

If your Strategy encourages you to Respond rather than Initiate, that does not make you passive or inactive. Think about it instead as an invitation to be on the lookout for a green light from the Universe to act in Alignment on an idea, inspiration or desire.

This may not feel like it comes naturally at first – it takes time to build the waiting muscle, to allow the thing to come to you, as we are usually conditioned to take massive action and initiate anything we want in life. Response takes active listening, attention and a willingness to be open to receiving external cues and acting on them when they come.

I cannot overstate the crucial role Strategy will play in your Human Design experiment. Think of your Strategy as the key to living your life in flow and feeling aligned to your energy – the portal into living with freedom and your most authentic self. When you're following your Strategy, you are living out your Design in real time and you're bound to be led deeper and more meaningfully through your Human Design journey, while simultaneously feeling more aligned in your relationships, purpose and other pursuits.

DISCOVER YOUR STRATEGY

Pull up your Human Design bodygraph. (If you don't have one yet, you can get yours at emmadunwoody.com now.)

Underneath the full-colour bodygraph image, you'll see your name, followed by your Human Design Type. Beneath your Type, you'll find your Strategy.

Once you've finished reading this introduction to Type and Strategy, go through the chapter until you find the section on your Strategy, where you'll find more details about living out your Strategy.

You'll also find other important information in the following pages that pertain to your Type and Strategy. You'll learn about:

- Your Signature Theme, which is the feeling you experience when you're living in Alignment with your Type and Strategy.
- Your Not-Self Theme, the feeling you'll experience when you're out of Alignment with your authentic self.
- How you can challenge your conditioning and blocks so that you can better embrace your Type and Strategy.
- How best to communicate based on your Type and Strategy.
- How you're Designed to thrive in relationships.
- How to develop meaningful self-care practices according to your Type and Strategy.

Throughout each Type section, you'll have the opportunity to reflect on and experiment with the knowledge presented. At the end of each Type section, you'll find a series of journal prompts to help you integrate what you've learned, reflect on how your Type and Strategy has already been at work in your life up until now and plan for the future with your Type and Strategy in mind.

CHAPTER INVITATION

You're probably going to want to skip ahead and read about your own Type first, and I get it. However, I urge you, once you've explored your own Type and Strategy, to come back and read through every section in this chapter. Taking the time to get to know all five types, not just your own, can have huge benefits.

First, it gives you a working knowledge of Human Design as a system. You'll better understand what sets you apart from other types, and what you have in common with them, too.

Second, representatives of each Type will be present in your life somewhere - whether that's at work, in your family or among your friends. Taking the time to understand every type will improve your relationships with the people you love - and the people you don't.

Finally, let me remind you - your Type is not a be-all-end-all definition of everything you are and aren't. You may very well find things that resonate with you in other sections, beyond your own Type. I encourage you to come to each Type with curiosity and openness to what you can learn about yourself, as well as others.

Human Design has helped me heal the relationship with my parents I didn't even know needed healing. Knowing their Design, including their shadows as well as their gifts, has helped me to gain a deeper understanding of how they function and why they do the things that they do. It's helped me to see them as souls here on a human journey too. And I can now see their amazing gifts and come to them for help with a specific thing. Seeing my parent's energetic blueprint, I love and value all parts of them so much more. I see more similarities between us that I hadn't before, even though they feel so obvious now. I feel like I 'get' them so much more. For example, my mum shares the same Profile as me, 1 / 3, and I totally see these qualities in her as I do in myself. Teaching her about her Design, even in her fifties, has brought her a sense of clarity, and a love for her strengths.

- Meg

7.
MANIFESTOR: YOUR TYPE AND STRATEGY MADE SIMPLE

Manifestors are trendsetters and trailblazers – you're on this earth to inspire action and change.

Manifestors make up around 9 per cent of the population.

THREE THINGS EVERY MANIFESTOR NEEDS TO KNOW:

- You're here to inspire *your* people into action, so be unapologetically *you*.
- You can be polarising, and this is a *good* thing.
- When your creative urge hits, do what you can to follow it.

THREE THINGS EVERY MANIFESTOR NEEDS TO DO:

- Stop apologising for being you and stop shutting down your power.
- Waste no more time trying to please others, or trying to be the version of you that makes them comfortable.
- Own your power.

HEY THERE, MANIFESTOR!

You are a one-of-a-kind force to be reckoned with. And your incredible passion and powerful energy aren't just incidental – they're part of you by Design.

Your unique Human Design empowers you to initiate action without the need for something external to respond to, just your innate creative energy that hits with impact and drive to make it manifest in the world. You're on this earth to inspire others into action, create change, lead by example and ignite creative sparks in those around you. And while your assertiveness might sometimes be misinterpreted as selfishness, it's actually what sets you apart and makes you a trailblazer.

Over the next few pages, we're going to unpack the essence of Manifestors – some of your dominant traits, your strategy for living in Alignment, your Signature Themes, the importance of embracing your authenticity and the keys to unlocking your full potential.

Remember, while this section speaks directly to Manifestors, it's worth a read regardless of your Type. The knowledge here can help you better understand and relate to the Manifestors in your life, so that you can both be the best versions of yourselves in relationships. And besides, you never know what little piece of wisdom might help guide you on your own Human Design experiment – even if the advice is aimed at a Type different from your own.

WHAT MAKES A MANIFESTOR?

Manifestors are defined by a unique energy configuration. You have a defined Throat Centre, but you do not have a defined Sacral Centre. This special setup allows you to be the initiator of action, without having to wait for external signals. You're the trailblazer, the trendsetter and the action-taker in the world. You are energetically independent, meaning you don't need others to make your dreams manifest; however, you want your people around you.

Manifestors' mission on this planet is crystal clear – you're here to ignite change, inspire others into action and lead by example. You possess a powerful creative urge that flows through you, driving you to take action. You're the rule breaker, the change maker and the paradigm shifter. You're Designed to be very unique, unapologetically yourself and to work with the creative flow from the Universe that moves freely through you as you bring creative inspiration into manifestation. Initiating is your jam, especially when it's aligned with your dreams.

WHAT MAKES A MANIFESTOR?

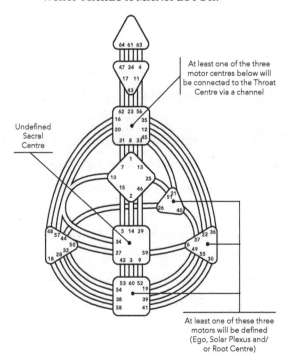

At least one of the three motor centres below will be connected to the Throat Centre via a channel

Undefined Sacral Centre

At least one of these three motors will be defined (Ego, Solar Plexus and/or Root Centre)

YOUR STRATEGY: INITIATE AND INFORM

Your Strategy is the most foundational building block for transforming your life through Human Design and living a life of freedom and authenticity. You can lean on your Strategy in every aspect of your life: from getting up in the morning to getting through your daily tasks and interacting with the world to going to bed at night. When you understand and follow your Strategy, growth happens. It may take some experimenting to figure out what living out your Strategy looks and feels like for you on a daily basis – remember, experimenting is what your Human Design journey is all about.

As a Manifestor, your strategy is to Initiate and Inform. Let's break it down:

Manifestors were put on this planet to inspire change. Initiation is the practice of creating something new, being internally inspired and then taking action to make the inspiration manifest in the world.

Simply put, you thrive when you make things happen and, crucially, when you *tell* people about the actions you're taking. People can only be inspired if they're made witness to the inspiring action.

Informing means declaring the direction of your energy. It's about communicating what you're up to, where you're headed and how you're feeling. However, it's important to understand that informing is *not* about asking for permission from the person you're speaking to. Instead, it's about keeping others informed so you are left alone and free to do your Manifestor thing. Informing takes practice; it doesn't come naturally to the Manifestor, because you fear others may try to stop you or get in your way when you Inform. However, the truth is Informing helps you find the community of people who you're meant to engage with. When you Inform those people who are here to be inspired into action by you, you *will* be inspired, and those who are not your people will drop away.

TRY THIS

By choosing this book, you've initiated a change in your life. So now it's time to step even more fully into Alignment through Informing.

Here's how: put this book down for a moment and take the time to tell someone in your life that you've begun your Human Design experiment.

Pay attention to how you feel when you share that information, and how the person you're sharing it with responds. Can you see them get excited for you, and maybe even inspired by you?

SIGNATURE THEME OF PEACE

Live in Alignment by embracing peace and learning from anger. As a Manifestor, your Signature Theme is *Peace*.

When you're in Alignment, you find peace in your body and environment. You're driven to create peaceful relationships and spaces, and you're pretty good at keeping the peace, even in high-stress situations.

NOT-SELF THEME OF ANGER

On the flipside, your Not-Self Theme is *Anger*. Anger tends to rear its head when your creative flow gets interrupted, or when you're forced into roles that stifle your creativity. The key here is to learn how to express anger resourcefully instead of bottling it up.

TRY THIS

To embrace your Signature Theme of Peace, make a mood board of images and words that make you feel peaceful. (Lean into your Strategy by telling someone you're making one.) Then keep your mood board in a place where you can see it regularly, like your office or in a prominent place in your home.

To release your Not-Self Theme of Anger, look again to your Strategy. Informing doesn't just mean telling other people what you're *going* to do. It also means Informing the people in your life of your feelings; it's about being the powerful communicator you are.

The next time you feel your Anger starting to boil over, call up a friend or loved one and share how you're feeling - and maybe consider Informing them about something you're going to do to find Peace.

YOUR RECONDITIONING JOURNEY

Many Manifestors commonly have to decondition from self-doubt, and recondition themselves to trust who they are and what they feel called to Initiate – even when their actions don't immediately make sense to others. Sound familiar?

As a kid, you might have realised that your energy impacted others, making you feel too independent, selfish or headstrong. You may have been afraid of being perceived as 'weird' or you might have felt very sensitive to rejection. As a result of these fears, authority figures in your life might have encouraged you to conform and make yourself small.

Today, you might find yourself playing small in your life – suppressing your energy to fit in, people-pleasing to avoid offending, being scared of doing something well and making others feel bad and uncomfortable or holding your tongue instead of speaking your truth. You might struggle with self-doubt. And because of your undefined Sacral Centre, which leads you to borrow energy from others, you might struggle to identify when enough is enough.

The good news is that you *can* recondition and realign yourself. The first step is to let go of beliefs that say, 'I'm too much,' 'I don't fit in,' or 'I'm weird.' Instead, embrace beliefs that lift you up and validate your strengths and gifts as a Manifestor.

MANTRAS FOR MANIFESTORS

I'm inspiring others through my authenticity and power.

Not everyone will like me; however, the ones who do will be inspired into action.

The more I Inform, the more flow, ease and grace I experience.

PRACTICAL TIPS FOR LIVING IN ALIGNMENT WITH YOUR MANIFESTOR TYPE

Communication

Manifestors thrive in clear, open communication. They are powerful communicators, after all. You respond best to open-ended questions, and you benefit not only from informing people about what you're doing, but also from being informed by others, too.

Never stifle what you need to say – speak up and share your truth.

Relationships

When it comes to relationships – both personal and professional – you're at your best when you have the freedom to follow your creative inspiration.

You don't like being told what to do, and you're definitely not here to conform, so you thrive when you surround yourself with people who let you do your thing.

Your energy, independence and powerful creative flow might make you feel like a bit of an outsider, but trust me, that's your superpower. In moments where you feel isolated, return to your Strategy: Initiate an action and Inform the people in your life of what you're doing. This is a way of reaching out and encouraging yourself at the same time.

Health and Well-Being

As non-Sacral beings, Manifestors' energy comes in bursts; it can be inconsistent. To get the most out of your energy, you need to work when your creative urge is flowing, and you need to rest, play and recover whenever you're not feeling that flow.

Make sure that you nourish yourself through hearty, fuelling meals when you're in creative mode and allow yourself to eat light when you're in resting mode.

A good night's sleep is essential for you. Try going to bed early *before* you even feel tired, and spending time daily in your own aura to cleanse and release others' energy.

JOURNAL PROMPTS FOR MANIFESTORS

Uncovering and healing the past:

- Where in my past have I been in Alignment with my Manifestor Type?
- Where in the past have I expressed my Not-Self Theme, Anger?
- What limiting beliefs in my past need to be healed and let go of so I can step into my power as a Manifestor?

Aligning with the now:

- What resonates with me about my Manifestor Type?
- What am I resisting about my Manifestor Type?

- What am I most curious to experiment with first regarding my Manifestor Type?

Creating the future:

- What three things am I going to do today to be more in Alignment with my Manifestor Type?
- How can my Manifestor Type support me in the future?
- How is life specifically better in the future because I'm living in Alignment as a Manifestor?

I've always felt misplaced in my family. I didn't feel loved or nurtured because I felt difficult to handle. It felt like I was ruffling feathers everywhere I turned.

Now that I've been living my Human Design experiment for a few years, I have to say it was life-changing when I found out I was a Manifestor. The repelling aura, the not liking being told what to do, not having as much energy as most people around me and being unlike many other people I knew permitted me to be my quirky self with my head held high.

I always knew I was here for something big and I'm still working on what that looks like. But the more I relax and ride my emotional waves, the better my life goes. I don't make snap decisions as often and see the results of not doing that. I have accepted my uniqueness and see it as a strength now. I feel like I've gone from the Ugly Duckling to the Swan through my experiment.

- Deb

8.
GENERATOR: YOUR TYPE AND STRATEGY MADE SIMPLE

Generators are builders – you thrive when you find and commit to work you truly love and that you feel makes a difference.

Generators make up around 38 per cent of the population.

THREE THINGS EVERY GENERATOR NEEDS TO KNOW:

- You are here to be lit up by the work you do.
- Your energy doesn't come from the mind, it comes from your Sacral Centre.
- Obligation will block your natural magnetism.

THREE THINGS EVERY GENERATOR NEEDS TO DO:

- Boundaries are your best friend; learn to say 'no' whenever it feels right, without needing an explanation.
- Stop overriding your instincts (aka your Sacral Response) with the mind.
- Move your body as often as you can.

HEY THERE, GENERATOR!

You're a passionate, committed worker who thrives whenever you're doing the things you love. You were Designed to centre your life around taking action in response to the things that light you up, and that's only the beginning – through doing what you love, you're making a crucial contribution to making this world a better place.

Generators are on this earth to be builders of a better world – this calling demands that you take what excites you, then build and expand upon it. Mastery of work and self-empowerment are at your fingertips, along with the ability to manifest and expand your horizons. However, it can be easy for Generators to get overloaded, to take on more than they can handle and to say 'yes' to too many things, instead of focusing on where they have the most passion and therefore can have the most impact. Your journey to living your best life means learning to respect your instinctual responses to people, places, opportunities and external cues. This is your Sacral telling you 'Yes, I have energy for this,' or 'No, I don't have energy for that.'

Over the next few pages, we're going to unpack the essence of Generators: some of your dominant traits, your strategy for living in Alignment, your Signature Themes, the importance of embracing your authenticity and the keys to unlocking your full potential.

Remember, while this section speaks directly to Generators, it's worth a read regardless of your Type. The knowledge here can help you better understand and relate to the Generators in your life, so that you can be the best version of yourselves in relationships. And besides, you never know what little piece of wisdom might help guide you on your own Human Design experiment – even if the advice is aimed at a Type different from your own.

WHAT MAKES A GENERATOR?

Generators possess a defined Sacral Centre, and this sets them apart from other Types. Unlike Manifestors, you do not have a defined Throat Centre, creating a unique dynamic that equips you to respond to external stimuli. Put simply, you have a killer gut instinct; you just have to learn to listen out for it, and act on it without letting the mind talk you out of it.

When you pay attention and remain present with your life and all that is happening in your environment, as well as recognising your immediate gut reaction to circumstances, you'll start to notice patterns in terms of what feels good and authentic for you. You'll learn to recognise the things you have energy for, versus the things you don't (remember, your Sacral Response gives you a 'yes' when you have the energy, and a 'no' when you don't). When you make choices that meaningfully reflect what your gut is telling you, you'll be unstoppable.

As a Generator, your mission in the world is to create life force energy for the planet by doing what lights you up. You're a master of work, and when you respond with a 'yes' that's authentic for you, your Sacral's immense power propels you to build, manifest and expand.

WHAT MAKES A GENERATOR?

Defined Sacral Centre

None of the motor centres (Root, Solar Plexus, Sacral and Ego) will be connected to the Throat Centre via a channel

YOUR STRATEGY: RESPOND

Your Strategy is the most foundational building block for transforming your life with Human Design. You can lean on your Strategy in every aspect of your life: from getting up in the morning to carrying out your daily tasks and interacting with the world to going to bed at night. When you understand and follow your Strategy, growth happens. It may take some experimenting to figure out what living out your Strategy looks and feels like for you, in your life, on a daily basis – but remember, experimenting is what your Human Design journey is all about.

As a Generator, your Strategy is to Respond. Let's talk about what that means. Generators thrive when taking action in direct response to something external to them, e.g. people, places, experiences and opportunities. Your Sacral Centre's engagement is the key, and its response will be provoked by something outside of you (i.e. not inspiration or intuition but something in your outer environment). That means you need to be present and open to observing, honouring and acting upon your gut response to the things that happen in your environment throughout your day.

Following your Strategy to Respond to your external environment, people, places and experiences is, ultimately, an exercise in identifying and following your truth.

TRY THIS

A big part of the Generator journey is learning to trust your instinctive sense of what's correct and what's *not* correct for you – this manifests in the body through a basic 'uh-huh' or 'uh-uh.' To get an idea of what that gut-level 'uh-huh' or 'uh-uh' feels like for you, ask a loved one to help you establish a baseline by asking you some of the following questions, and inviting you to answer on the spot with a simple 'uh-huh' or 'uh-uh' response.

Is your name [blank]?

Were you born on [blank]?

Do you live in [blank]?

Did you have a coffee this morning?

Are you hungry?

Pay attention to how your body feels when you respond with 'uh-huh's and 'uh-uh's to the questions.

As you get familiar with your 'uh-huh' and 'uh-uh' response, you can move on to bigger questions, like . . .

Do you feel lit up by your work?

Are you satisfied by your life?

Are you working towards the things you want?

SIGNATURE THEME OF SATISFACTION

Live in Alignment by embracing satisfaction and learning from frustration. As a Generator, your Signature Theme is *Satisfaction*.

When you operate from Alignment, you experience a deep contentment in your body and surroundings. This satisfaction stems from a job well done, and it can manifest in small or large victories.

NOT-SELF THEME OF FRUSTRATION

Meanwhile, your Not-Self Theme is *Frustration*.

Frustration can often creep in when you overthink instead

of trusting your Sacral Response. It's a sign of disconnection from your natural flow. Whenever you feel energetically stuck and frustrated, the best remedy is to move your body to release the pent-up energy.

TRY THIS

Spend the next few days documenting moments when you feel Satisfied versus moments when you feel Frustrated.

Make note of what happened just before you felt Frustrated or Satisfied with each response, and develop an awareness of environments and situations that trigger Frustration and Satisfaction. Plan to consciously put boundaries in place where Frustration is triggered and do more of what feels Satisfying.

Where you can't avoid Frustration, look at what is coming up within you. What is the Frustration trying to show you?

YOUR RECONDITIONING JOURNEY

Generators are often conditioned to say 'yes' to everything. This conditioning disregards the Sacral's guidance and contributes to having very few boundaries, which can lead to feeling resentful, exhausted and result in functional burnout.

WHAT IS FUNCTIONAL BURNOUT?

Functional burnout is what happens when you're still going through all the motions of work and life, even though you're feeling completely exhausted, overworked and out of Alignment. You may feel like you no longer have any passion for your work or life; you're just living Groundhog Day and going through the motions. It's an issue that regularly affects Generators and Manifesting Generators when they haven't recognised an external cue to stop and rest.

The best way to avoid functional burnout is to learn how to recognise and honour your Sacral Response. This section, as well as the Manifestor, Manifesting Generator and Sacral Authority sections of this book, can help you do that.

Because you've been conditioned to trample over your own boundaries, you may regularly experience challenges around feeling used. You might have a fear of rejection if you say 'no', and because you're conditioned to say 'yes' to everything, you probably struggle to identify what truly lights you up.

But don't let yourself get discouraged by your conditioning. You *can* recondition to live in Alignment with your Design.

The first step to reconditioning is to let go of unresourceful beliefs like, 'I must do everything myself' and 'I can, so I should.' Replace these with empowering beliefs that recognise the value of your powerful energy and your right to say 'no' when something doesn't light you up.

MANTRAS FOR GENERATORS

My powerful energy matters and I deserve to say 'no' to whatever doesn't light me up.

When I say an aligned 'no,' it's a gift for me AND the other person.

I follow my greatest excitement in every moment.

I am building the new world, guided by what lights me up.

PRACTICAL TIPS FOR GENERATORS

Communication

Encourage the people in your life to use yes/no questions with you – you're Designed to break down information into something your Sacral can respond to with a 'Yes, I have energy for this' or 'No, I don't have energy for this.'

If yes/no answers aren't possible, you can benefit from breaking down complex questions into smaller, more manageable pieces.

You love to talk about what lights you up, so drop the complaining about what you do not have energy for and start talking about all the things – big and small – that light you up.

Remember that your most authentic and powerful communication occurs when it naturally flows in response to your external environment, people, places and experiences. This response is where you can fully harness what is authentic for you and make the most of your Human Design as a Generator.

Relationships

In relationships, you thrive when your commitment to your work – to the things that light you up – is appreciated and respected. You also need to be around people who respect your communication style and are willing and able to do the work to adapt.

You need to have solid boundaries in your relationships, otherwise you will end up taking too much responsibility for them, leading to resentment.

Having a partner who honours your Generator process without judgement is crucial for your well-being. You need to be free to follow what lights you up without having to explain or justify yourself.

Sexual and intimate energy is a large part of your Sacral/Generator energy. Practise balancing your intimate life and your work life, rather than indulging too far in one or the other.

Health and Well-Being

Your energy is available when your Sacral says 'uh-huh', so work the amount that feels correct for you, but remember to balance rest and play with the work you love – Generators need time off too.

Take care to fuel your body with hearty meals and regular snacks – your Sacral Centre needs a lot of energy!

To stay connected to your Sacral, it's important that you use your energy up each day. Move your body by doing something you enjoy – keep going until you feel fatigued.

Get better rest by going to bed when you're ready and able to go straight to sleep.

JOURNAL PROMPTS FOR GENERATORS

Uncovering and healing the past:

- Where in my past have I been in Alignment with my Generator Type?
- Where in the past have I expressed my Not-Self Theme, Frustration?
- What limiting beliefs in my past need to be healed and let go of so I can step into my power as a Generator?

Aligning with the now:

- What resonates with me about my Generator Type?
- What am I resisting about my Generator Type?
- What am I most curious to experiment with first regarding my Generator Type?

Creating the future:

- What three things am I going to do today to be more in Alignment with my Generator Type?
- How can my Generator Type support me in the future?
- How is life specifically better in the future because I'm living in Alignment as a Generator?

9.
MANIFESTING GENERATOR: YOUR TYPE AND STRATEGY MADE SIMPLE

Manifesting Generators are here to demonstrate human potential; you inspire and impact others by living your most authentic life.

Manifesting Generators make up around 32 per cent of the population.

THREE THINGS EVERY MANIFESTING GENERATOR NEEDS TO KNOW:

- You are here to demonstrate human potential; you can be superhuman.
- You are a non-linear being – being all over the place is your magic.
- You too need rest, recovery and play.

THREE THINGS EVERY MANIFESTING GENERATOR NEEDS TO DO:

- Give yourself permission to be too much, take up space and be unapologetically *you*!
- Follow your multiple passions.
- Trust the mess, breaking and remaking: you're here to build something better and remarkable.

HEY THERE, MANIFESTING GENERATOR!

You're the kind of person who sparks curiosity and attraction from others wherever you go. You've probably been told it's extraordinary how you do what you do – and that's exactly how you're meant to be! Your knack for standing out in a crowd doesn't make you 'weird' – it's an integral element of your Human Design.

Manifesting Generators embody a hybrid type, blending the characteristics of both Manifestors and Generators – so go back and read more about these Types, too.

Manifesting Generators are non-linear people, multi-passionate, who will never follow one singular path, especially in their work, where their responses are internally governed through the Sacral. This internal rhythm, combined with a swift, unconventional approach, can sometimes ruffle other people's feathers. However, learning to embrace your unique and powerful impact is integral to your success.

Over the next few pages, we're going to unpack the essence of Manifesting Generators: some of your dominant traits, your strategy for living in Alignment, your Signature Themes, the importance of embracing your authenticity and the keys to unlocking your full potential.

Remember, while this section speaks directly to Manifesting Generators, it's worth a read regardless of your Type. The knowledge here can help you better understand and relate to the Manifesting Generators in your life, so that you can both be the best versions of yourselves in relationships. And besides, you never know what little piece of wisdom might help guide you on your own Human Design experiment – even if the advice is aimed at a Type different to your own.

WHAT MAKES A MANIFESTING GENERATOR?

Manifesting Generators' energy combines some aspects of both Manifestors and Generators. Your unique Design includes a defined Sacral Centre (just like Generators) *and* a defined Throat Centre, the defining characteristic of Manifestors. This makes you energetically independent like Manifestors, i.e. you don't need other people's energy to manifest; however, you want your people around you.

Your defined Sacral is an incredible energy source that propels you through life. This distinction sets you apart, allowing you to harness a specific kind of power and vitality that's palpable in your presence. Coupled with your defined Throat Centre, it signifies a direct channel between your energy and your ability to articulate and manifest desires into reality.

This non-linear energy translates into a way of being that doesn't follow the conventional step-by-step progression. Your internal guidance system, coupled with your rapid responsiveness, propels you to move swiftly and at times jump ahead without taking all the steps others will have to take to get the same results. It's a fluid, adaptive and instinctual way of operating that distinguishes you, allowing for multipassionate exploration and expression.

WHAT MAKES A MANIFESTING GENERATOR?

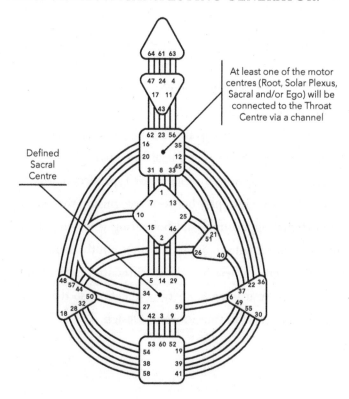

At least one of the motor centres (Root, Solar Plexus, Sacral and/or Ego) will be connected to the Throat Centre via a channel

Defined Sacral Centre

YOUR STRATEGY: RESPOND AND INFORM

Your Strategy is the most foundational building block for transforming your life through Human Design. You can lean on your Strategy in every aspect of your life: from getting up in the morning to carrying out your daily tasks and interacting with the world to going to bed at night. When you understand and follow your Strategy, growth happens. It may take some experimenting to figure out what living out your Strategy looks and feels like for you, in your life, on a daily basis – remember, experimenting is what your Human Design journey is all about.

As a Manifesting Generator, your Strategy is to Respond and Inform. Let's break down what that means:

This Strategy is deeply rooted in your ability to respond to your environment with your internal Sacral energy.

You need to patiently await something in your external environment that aligns with your Sacral Response (see the 'uh-huh' and 'uh-uh' exercise from the Generator Type section, page 93).

It's a delicate interplay between recognising the resonance of an external opportunity and honouring your gut responses. Moreover, your innate ability to inform is not the same as seeking permission; rather, it's about authentic expression and declaration of your internal energy's direction, so that you can foster Alignment with your inherent Design.

TRY THIS

Keep a journal this week of all the opportunities that come your way and how your Sacral responds to them. Did you have energy for them or not? Reflect on the things you had energy for and what you didn't - this is your Sacral guiding you to greater Alignment. From there, be sure to inform people in your life of your plans - this helps you commit, and cues others to advocate for or pass on your endeavours.

SIGNATURE THEMES OF SATISFACTION AND PEACE

Live in Alignment by embracing Satisfaction and Peace, and learn from Anger and Frustration. As a Manifesting Generator, your Signature Themes are Satisfaction and Peace.

Satisfaction looks and feels different for everybody, so take some time to become aware of how you experience it: you might gain Satisfaction through completing a task efficiently, from being aligned with your true calling, through the joy of engaging in diverse activities that resonate with your multipassionate nature, all of the above or something else entirely. This Theme acts as a compass, indicating when you're in synch with your authentic self.

You also thrive when you feel at Peace. This could be mentally, physically and/or emotionally, through the peaceful internal or external environment you feel free to create. That Peace wants to be present in your relationships, in the physical spaces you occupy or in moments of internal harmony. When you have a sense of inner Peace, it signifies your Alignment and serves as a guide to gauge whether you're in synch with your Design.

NOT-SELF THEMES OF FRUSTRATION AND ANGER

On the flipside, your Not-Self Themes are Frustration and Anger.

Frustration and Anger are indicators of misalignment, prompting you to pay attention to elements that disrupt your natural flow. Frustration often arises when you're caught up in over analysis or when your natural responses are questioned or disregarded. Anger, on the other hand, emerges when your creative urges are interrupted or when external pressures stifle your authentic flow. These themes signal when there's a deviation from your natural state, urging you to realign with your authentic self.

TRY THIS

Tune into your Sacral Response and learn more about what people, places and experiences initiate your Signature and Not-Self Themes this week by regularly asking yourself the following yes/no questions:

Do I feel satisfied right now?

Do I feel at peace right now?

Do I feel frustrated right now?

Do I feel angry right now?

Whenever the answer to any of these questions is 'yes', observe what happened externally right before you felt that way, and explore how that experience may have triggered the feeling you're experiencing.

YOUR RECONDITIONING JOURNEY

As a Manifesting Generator, you've likely been conditioned by society and authority figures to conform, to repress your big energy and to accept any and every responsibility that gets heaped on you. Over time, this leads to feelings of resentment and keeps you from living in Alignment and forces you to work harder and do more. Overcoming these unresourceful beliefs involves recognising your immense potential and transcending fears of being perceived as 'too much'.

You've probably also experienced some shame about the way you approach tasks, and been conditioned over time to be a perfectionist. You might fear quitting, undertaking tasks one at a time and following linear modes of being and working that don't align with your Design.

The conditioning you've encountered might have urged you to tone yourself down, to play small with your innate abilities and to fit in and conform to societal expectations. The pressure to hold back, to conform to conventional expectations, might have led you to take on more than your fair share of responsibilities, often resulting in feelings of resentment and a misalignment with your authentic self.

Reconditioning involves shedding these limiting beliefs, acknowledging your vast potential and embracing your bigness without fear of being perceived as too much.

For you, the reconditioning process is about shedding the layers of family and societal pressures that have led to self-doubt and the suppression of your innate energy. Your reconditioning journey means embracing your non-linear energy and your true capabilities, and cultivating an understanding that being authentically 'you' is not only acceptable but essential for your Alignment and well-being.

MANTRAS FOR MANIFESTING GENERATORS

My powerful energy matters and I deserve to say 'no' to whatever doesn't light me up.

I follow my greatest excitement in every moment.

I am superhuman and deserve to experience my greatest potential.

I'm inspiring others through my messiness, passion, authenticity and power to follow my own unique path.

PRACTICAL TIPS FOR LIVING IN ALIGNMENT WITH YOUR MANIFESTING GENERATOR TYPE

Communication

You communicate most effectively when you're asked yes/no questions that allow you to respond authentically from the Sacral rather than from the mind.

When a topic doesn't lend itself to yes/no questions, try deconstructing the issue into its smallest parts, so you can address things one at a time.

Relationships

When it comes to cultivating successful relationships as a Manifesting Generator, you need to surround yourself with people who understand and champion your distinct work processes.

In relationships, you need the freedom to be you and to follow your own path. Being energetically independent can mean you are less likely to need others; however, you will still want others to share your journey with.

Asking for help is an important muscle to build for you as it most likely will not come naturally.

In relationships you will thrive when your partner appreciates the work you do.

Health and Well-Being

Your well-being as a Manifesting Generator is intricately linked to recognising and honouring your Sacral Responses.

You will tend to have a big appetite; the Sacral needs a lot of fuel – especially up until your forties.

As a Manifesting Generator, daily physical movement is very important for your energy. If you feel stuck, move your body. If you feel sad, move your body. If you need energy, move your body.

It is important for you to take time to wind down before bed, as it takes time to settle your nervous system; you're like a Ferrari – moving all day at great speed, but your engine doesn't begin to recover until it cools.

Pursue activities that genuinely ignite your passion and give yourself permission to follow your own rhythm, even if it doesn't match what others around you are doing.

JOURNAL PROMPTS FOR MANIFESTING GENERATORS

Uncovering and healing the past:

- Where in my past have I been in Alignment with my Manifesting Generator Type?
- Where in the past have I expressed my Not-Self Themes, Anger and Frustration?

- What limiting beliefs in my past need to be healed and let go of so I can step into my power as a Manifesting Generator?

Aligning with the now:

- What resonates with me about my Manifesting Generator Type?
- What am I resisting about my Manifesting Generator Type?
- What am I most curious to experiment with first regarding my Manifesting Generator Type?

Creating the future:

- What three things am I going to do today to be more in Alignment with my Manifesting Generator Type?
- How can my Manifesting Generator Type support me in the future?
- How is life specifically better in the future because I'm living in Alignment as a Manifesting Generator?

10.
PROJECTOR: YOUR TYPE AND STRATEGY MADE SIMPLE

Projectors are thoughtful and wise – you're here to help others find their way and use their energy most efficiently.

Projectors make up about 20 per cent of the population.

THREE THINGS EVERY PROJECTOR NEEDS TO KNOW:

- Invitations will arrive when you have the energy to fulfil them.
- You're at your best one-on-one, though you can do well one-to-many.
- You have specific people you're here to guide.

THREE THINGS EVERY PROJECTOR NEEDS TO DO:

- Rest, recover, learn and play when there are no invitations on the table.
- Stop taking people's disinterest personally and work on your wisdom instead.
- Surround yourself with people who value your wisdom, opinion and guidance – people who see and acknowledge you.

HEY THERE, PROJECTOR!

You're a wise, thoughtful guide to others. Your perspective and empathy are sought after, and you're uniquely Designed to guide others on their own journeys.

You're here to observe, understand and offer advice on how you see others using their energy, to share efficiencies and to offer advice on how they can do things differently, better and more effectively and thrive. While it can be challenging to learn how and when to share your wisdom, and how to navigate the difficult feelings that come up when your guidance is not appreciated, know that your unique point of view is a critical puzzle piece for a better world. When you find the right places to offer it, you make an incredible, lasting impact.

Over the next few pages, we're going to unpack the essence of Projectors: some of your dominant traits, your strategy for living in Alignment, your Signature Themes, the importance of embracing your authenticity and the keys to unlocking your full potential.

Remember, while this section speaks directly to Projectors, it's worth a read regardless of your Type. The knowledge here can help you better understand and relate to the Projectors in your life, so that you can both be the best versions of yourselves in a relationship. And besides, you never know what little piece of wisdom might help guide you on your own Human Design experiment – even if the advice is aimed at a Type different from your own.

WHAT MAKES A PROJECTOR?

When you look at your bodygraph, you may notice that your Sacral and Throat Centres are undefined. These are the qualities that define you as a Projector, and that makes you uniquely qualified to encourage others through deep understanding and thoughtful guidance.

In fact, your entire mission in life is to guide others so that they can use their own energy most efficiently. With your help, all the Human Design Types can pursue their own purposes, and together we can all work towards better lives for ourselves and a better world for everyone.

However, it's important to understand how and when your guidance will be helpful, and to hold back your advice until you're invited to share it. More about that next.

WHAT MAKES A PROJECTOR?

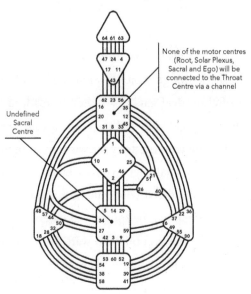

None of the motor centres (Root, Solar Plexus, Sacral and Ego) will be connected to the Throat Centre via a channel

Undefined Sacral Centre

YOUR STRATEGY: WAIT FOR AN INVITATION

Your Strategy is the most foundational building block for transforming your life through Human Design. You can lean on your Strategy in every aspect of your life: from getting up in the morning to getting through your daily tasks and interacting with the world to going to bed at night. When you understand and follow your Strategy, growth happens. It may take some experimenting to figure out what living out your Strategy looks and feels like for you, in your life, on a daily basis – remember, experimenting is what your Human Design journey is all about.

As a Projector, your strategy is to Wait for the Invitation. Let's unpack that. As you may have guessed, Waiting for the Invitation means that you need to conserve your energy and your guidance until you are asked to give it.

That's not always an easy thing, but it's crucial: if you don't wait to be asked, your guidance (even when it's completely right) is likely to fall on deaf ears. It's better, instead, to wait for the people who really get you, and respond to your energy, to seek you out and invite you to offer your wisdom to them.

Your Strategy challenges you to know the value of your own wisdom; to trust that your guidance will be needed, that it matters and that you will be sought out when the time is right.

When you're brave enough to wait, the opportunities that come your way are much more likely to match your energetic capacity and be best suited to your expertise.

Just because you're waiting, that doesn't mean you get to be passive. When no invitations are on the table, invest in yourself: resting, playing and learning are all methods of deepening your own wisdom, so that when the invitation does come, you're ready and primed to share. Think about it like allowing a flower to bloom in its own time: your focus should be on nurturing your own wisdom, so that when conditions are right, your knowledge and guidance can flower for the right person.

TRY THIS

Fun fact: Projectors were not made to work 9-5. In fact, you're most efficient when you work about three hours a day and then take plenty of time for rest, play and personal reflection.

This suggestion may sound unrealistic, but, as a Projector you have the ability to do *more* with *less*. One of your superpowers is to find efficiencies, and when you use them to do more with less, then you can honour your energy.

For a week, focus on efficiency. Brainstorm how can you do things better and faster, with the intention of reducing your work time.

Only do work that you're invited to do - don't let yourself take on tasks or volunteer to offer guidance that you haven't been expressly invited to weigh in on.

As you shed tasks that weren't meant for you, and your working time shrinks, pay attention to what blooms in the space you make in your life. What new, aligned opportunities arise as a result of taking space for yourself? Continue the experiment beyond a week if you can.

SIGNATURE THEME OF SUCCESS

Live in Alignment by embracing Success and learning from Bitterness. As a Projector, your Signature Theme is Success.

You experience a real sense of Success when you can see how your wisdom contributes to the Success of others. You really thrive and feel successful when others recognise the value you bring to the table. However, you don't need other people to tap into that sense of Success: simply by recognising yourself and taking time to reflect on your achievements, you can also experience Success.

NOT-SELF THEME OF BITTERNESS

On the flipside, your Not-Self Theme is Bitterness.

When your wisdom goes unrecognised or unacknowledged, you may resent the people you advised and feel bitter about the experience. It's crucial to address this bitterness and understand if it's preventing you from recognising your worth. Pay attention to when your wisdom is ignored because you did not follow your Strategy and wait for an invitation.

TRY THIS

Start keeping a log of compliments and notes of appreciation you receive from people who invited you to share your expertise, guidance and wisdom. Go back through appreciative emails, social media comments, positive performance reviews and thank you notes you've received to really build out your collection.

Any time you feel Bitterness start to creep into your mind, return to this log of Successes as proof that, in the right hands, your wisdom is deeply valued and appreciated.

Also pay attention to what happened right before you felt Bitterness – were you offering unsolicited advice? Were you seeking external validation? Pay attention to these behaviours and let them go – choose invitations and validating yourself instead.

YOUR RECONDITIONING JOURNEY

The journey of a Projector involves shedding self-doubt and the need for attention and validation, and reconditioning yourself to trust who you are, what you see and what you're here to give. In childhood, you might have felt pressured to downplay what you knew and saw, but now is the time to let go of limiting beliefs and recognise your strength. Conditioned Projectors often over-work themselves in a desperate attempt to feel seen and acknowledged. Because of this need to be recognised, Projectors may engage in unresourceful attention-seeking and pushiness, and often experience burnout and low self-worth.

Conditioned Projectors are often ruled by fear: fear of not being seen and heard, fear of being perceived as lazy or passive. A lot of this fear stems from the fact that your Design is so different to the majority of the world. You need lots of time, space, and discipline to wait, which can be frustrating in a world that likes to move at breakneck speed. The pace of the world, dominated by high-energy Types, might make you feel like you need to force and hustle to keep up. Remember, your unique energy has its own rhythm, and success doesn't solely depend on constant action. Less is more with you.

To start to overcome the challenges of your conditioning, you need to address your fears of not being seen or heard, by committing to seeing and hearing yourself – by recognising your own value, you can combat your fear of being overlooked, to validate yourself and your wisdom. You also need to stop overworking on the wrong things, and release the misconception that success comes from constant action.

To let go of unresourceful beliefs and affirm the value of your wisdom, you need to release any negative beliefs about who you are. Let go of thought patterns like, *I need to work hard to be successful and worthy* or *People don't listen to me* or *My worth is in how much I can do for others*. Instead, work towards owning positive new beliefs that highlight the value of your unique Design.

MANTRAS FOR PROJECTORS

My wisdom is valuable, and I only share it when it is curiously invited.

When I see and acknowledge myself first, others follow.

I am here to guide my specific people, and I save my energy for them.

My alone time is of the greatest importance to me and it amplifies my ability to serve.

PRACTICAL TIPS FOR LIVING IN ALIGNMENT WITH YOUR PROJECTOR TYPE

Communication

Projectors thrive in open, meaningful dialogue and when their wisdom is appreciated and invited. Invite the people in your life to ask you open-ended questions; this allows for the depth, exploration and meaningful connection that you value in conversation. It's also the best way to tease out your unique wisdom, giving you opportunities to share the patterns, connections and efficiencies you see arising through your unique talent for observation.

Ask for the recognition you need. While it's important for Projectors to move beyond a dependence on external validation, it can also be empowering to be upfront about your need for acknowledgement and recognition. Be open about how these affirmations contribute to your well-being.

Relationships

When it comes to being in relationships with others – your friends, family, colleagues and acquaintances – you need a healthy balance of you-time and meaningful opportunities for connection.

You have a gift for seeing deeply into others – this is a gift to give and requires boundaries, so be sure to give your energy to those who invite it and who you feel excited to share with.

Express the importance of invitations and acknowledgement in your relationships. When these elements are present, your wisdom flows more naturally, enriching the connection.

Also encourage the people in your life to understand you are here to be seen and acknowledged; let people know it's like a love language to you.

Finally, make sure you have good boundaries around your you-time. You must have space to recharge; that might be alone time, being in nature, reading, etc. Be sure that you communicate your need for time out with others, otherwise you will get drawn along with other people's energy and desires. Your energy fluctuates, and understanding this rhythm is crucial for maintaining healthy relationships.

Health and Well-Being

Thanks to your undefined Sacral Centre, you probably experience fluctuating highs and lows in your energy levels, often depending on what – and who – is around you. Because of this, you need to know what gives you energy and what takes your energy, and you need to get comfortable following your own rhythm, even if it seems at odds with other people in your life.

When it comes to fuelling your body with food, focus on eating light and only when you feel hungry.

Remember that less is more in everything you do, so don't overdo it at work, at the gym or in the yoga studio. Spend time in nature, drink water, meditate, dance – anything that revives and resets your energy.

Build in comfort systems for when you are running low on energy: know who on your working team you can rely on, or who you might ask to help you with the kids. Build in a take-away budget, or have easy meals on hand.

You also need quality sleep. Always try to go to bed before you feel tired, and wind down by reading, journalling or meditating. If you can, sleep alone, even if it's only once a week.

JOURNAL PROMPTS FOR PROJECTORS

Uncovering and healing the past:

- Where in my past have I been in Alignment with my Projector Type?
- Where in the past have I expressed my Not-Self Theme, Bitterness?
- What limiting beliefs in my past need to be healed and let go of so I can step into my power as a Projector?

Aligning with the now:

- What resonates with me about my Projector Type?
- What am I resisting about my Projector Type?
- What am I most curious to experiment with first regarding my Projector Type?

Creating the future:

- What three things am I going to do today to be more in Alignment with my Projector Type?
- How can my Projector Type support me in the future?
- How is life specifically better in the future because I'm living in Alignment as a Projector?

11.
REFLECTOR: YOUR TYPE AND STRATEGY MADE SIMPLE

Reflectors are here to amplify energy, see energy deeply and bring awareness to others.

Reflectors make up about 1 per cent of the population.

THREE THINGS EVERY REFLECTOR NEEDS TO KNOW:

- To make decisions that are correct for you, Reflectors need to be in the right place, with the right people and take their time.
- You are powerful and you *do* know who you are! Your ability to see, sense, read and work with subtle energy is extraordinary.

- Take your time – you are a time lord, you have all the time in the world.

THREE THINGS EVERY REFLECTOR NEEDS TO DO:

- Spend time with people who are curious to get to know *you* on a deeper level.
- Be disciplined about the people you hang out with and the places you go – they are creating your experience.
- Trust your power, trust your timing and believe in the ever-changing *you*, because your heart and soul knows where you're going.

HEY THERE, REFLECTOR!

You're sensitive, observant and deeply in tune with the energy of others – and you were Designed to bring these much-needed gifts to the world.

Your Design offers something truly special to others: the opportunity for them to see themselves and their future potential more clearly, and in doing so, to align more authentically with who they are.

You find Alignment when you're paying attention to, and making decisions in Alignment with, how people, places and experiences make you feel. You're reflecting back to the people around you, who they're being and what they're doing. This gives them the opportunity to see themselves with clarity and then make changes accordingly – to clarify their vision or celebrate where they're at.

If people, places and experiences do not feel good for you, then it may be time to move on. Maybe those around you are not taking responsibility for their behaviour and projecting it onto you. Maybe you don't feel seen or understood because others are lost in their own reflection – this means it's time to move on to a different relationship, group or job.

Your energy and way of being may feel transient, shapeshifting and changeable due to the way you take in other people's energy and amplify it. Your energy takes time and patience to master, but trust that people need you to reflect the truth of who they are back to them.

Over the next few pages, we're going to unpack the essence of Reflectors: some of your dominant traits, your Strategy for living in Alignment, your Signature Themes, the importance of embracing your authenticity and the keys to unlocking your full potential.

Remember, while this section speaks directly to Reflectors, it's worth a read regardless of your Type. The knowledge here can help you better understand and relate to the Reflectors in your life, so that you can both be the best versions of yourselves in relationships. And besides, you never know what little piece of wisdom might help guide you on your own Human Design experiment – even if the advice is aimed at a Type different from your own.

WHAT MAKES A REFLECTOR?

Reflectors are the rarest Human Design Type, and they are defined by having no defined Centres. This results in greater energetic inconsistency. Unlike the other four Types, your consistency doesn't stem from the usual energy Centres. Instead, your energy comes from the themes intricately woven into your Design and the rhythmic dance of the 28-day moon cycle.

WHAT MAKES A REFLECTOR?

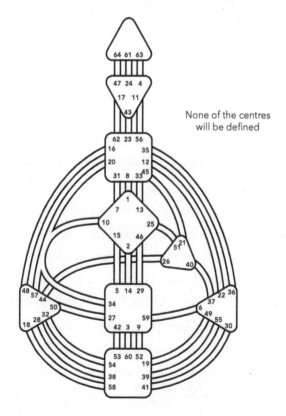

None of the centres
will be defined

Unlike other Types, Reflectors are less likely to have other people's energy stick with them; instead, they observe, feel and reflect it, gaining a unique insight into the potential of other people and the planet.

Your mission is to help other people see their potential, and to reflect how the people around you can contribute to a better world. You are here to mirror and demonstrate truth, to see energy deeply, to foretell and reflect the untapped potential within a community or individual.

YOUR STRATEGY: FOLLOW THE 28-DAY MOON CYCLE

Your Strategy is the most foundational building block for transforming your life through Human Design. You can lean on your Strategy in every aspect of your life: from getting up in the morning to carrying out your daily tasks and interacting with the world to going to bed at night. When you understand and follow your Strategy, growth happens. It may take some experimenting to figure out what living out your Strategy looks and feels like for you, in your life, on a daily basis – remember, experimenting is what your Human Design journey is all about.

As a Reflector, your Strategy is to Follow the 28-Day Moon Cycle. Let's unpack that. Put simply, you need to become intimately aware of how your energy shifts based on how the moon moves through your chart. The lunar cycle becomes your compass, offering short-lived definitions as the moon moves through each gate. Slowing down, feeling deeply and sampling life will allow your unique decisions to surface gradually, creating a harmonious synchrony with the Universe.

The most important thing for you as a Reflector is to slow down, take your time and reject the pressure to decide, act, deliver and respond on someone else's timeline.

TRY THIS

Track how you feel throughout the moon cycle.

Starting with the next new moon, on each of the following 28 days, note in your journal how much energy you have out of ten each day and the significant energies you feel, i.e. fear, joy, love, curiosity, etc. Also record how you feel around the people you spend time with each day.

By taking the time to track the patterns of your energy, you'll become more aware of how much your environment is dictating your choices and finally learn to spend time on your own, feeling what it is to be you in each moment.

SIGNATURE THEME OF SURPRISE

Live in Alignment by embracing surprise and learning from disappointment. As a Reflector, your Signature Theme is Surprise.

You find a deep sense of joyful wonder when you discover potential in yourself and others. You treasure the surprises of potential fulfilled, and you thrive when you get to share the potential that lies within others.

NOT-SELF THEME OF DISAPPOINTMENT

As a Reflector, your Not-Self Theme is Disappointment.

Disappointment surfaces when you witness unmet potential and are confronted by what could have been. It can lead you to feel lost and to experience a lack of trust in yourself, others and even the Universe.

TRY THIS

Make a list of small ways you can celebrate surprising moments of revealed potential: can you pick a flower, listen to your favourite song or treat yourself to help you prolong the pleasure of the Surprise?

Meanwhile, whenever you feel Disappointed, remind yourself of the untapped potential still waiting to be discovered. Things may not have worked out this time, but there is always new potential around the corner. Trust that Surprise will replace Disappointment soon enough.

Your Reconditioning Journey

Conditioned Reflectors often find themselves transforming into chameleons, adapting to others' needs and losing their true essence in the process. Because you're Designed to reflect, you can become so lost in mirroring others that you completely lose sight of who you are and what you need.

As a child, you might have been praised for your ability to perfectly blend in with others, bowing to everyone else's needs except your own. You might have felt undue pressure to constantly adapt, and a destabilising sense of not knowing who you are when you're not with other people.

But constant self-transformation and people-pleasing is exhausting and ultimately obscures your profound gift of perceiving, feeling, knowing and reflecting subtle energies. You're not here to blend in with others; you're here to help the people in your life recognise themselves more fully, so they can stand out in their own right and so can you. Your deep empathy and ability to reflect others back to themselves does not doom you to lose yourself – you simply have to know how to find what makes you you, and foster it.

To move towards authenticity, Reflectors must release unresourceful beliefs and directives like, 'I need to hurry up,' or 'I don't know who I am because I'm different depending on who I'm with,' or 'I can't be myself. I don't know myself.'

Instead, develop beliefs that celebrate your superpower as a Reflector. Recognise that the gift you give others is a remarkable and singular part of who you are.

MANTRAS FOR REFLECTORS

I am a powerful mirror, and therefore I choose powerful people to reflect.

When I allow the ebb and flow of my me-ness, I experience surprise and delight.

Subtle energy is my jam; I trust what I see, feel, know and reflect.

I show people their truth.

PRACTICAL TIPS FOR LIVING IN ALIGNMENT WITH YOUR REFLECTOR TYPE

Communication

Reflectors thrive on open-ended questions and the space to reflect and discuss. You may need to have the same conversation a number of times over a few days or even weeks before you come to clarity – this is perfectly aligned for you. You operate best when you're asked lots of thoughtful questions about yourself and your experience; this makes you feel seen instead of unseen in the reflections of others.

You also communicate through subtle energy, how you feel, the 'vibe' – slowing down so you can absorb and read the subtle energy is important, and then you notice body language, what's not being said and what's going on in the surrounding energy.

Relationships

As Reflectors have inconsistent energy, you need to surround yourself with people who are more than happy to give you space and time to restore your energy levels.

In relationships you need to be with a person who understands your process takes time. You also want to choose friends and partners who encourage you to make your own choices, rather than taking advantage of your Reflecting nature.

Reflectors can commonly experience codependency because the relationships in their life provide consistency and safety. If this resonates with you, then look into healing your codependency: realise that you need to know what your needs are and fulfil them first before worrying about others.

Health and Well-Being

You need lots of rest, so don't overwork yourself – in your job, social life or through physical activity. Take regular breaks, as many as possible, and engage with tasks that allow you to take your time. Don't overdo it at work, at the gym or in the yoga studio – trust your body's feedback.

Your appetite may fluctuate depending on who you're with and your environment. Pay attention to how you're feeling and what nourishes you versus what starves or overstuffs you.

Set boundaries that allow you to get lots of sleep. Sleep alone if you can, even if it's once a week.

JOURNAL PROMPTS FOR REFLECTORS

Uncovering and healing the past:

* Where in the past have I been in Alignment with my Reflector Type?
* Where in the past have I expressed my Not-Self Theme, Disappointment?
* What limiting beliefs in my past need to be healed and let go of so I can step into my power as a Reflector?

Aligning with the now:

* What resonates with me about my Reflector Type?
* What am I resisting about my Reflector Type?
* What am I most curious to experiment with first regarding my Reflector Type?

Creating the future:

* What three things am I going to do today to be more in Alignment with my Reflector Type?
* How can my Reflector Type support me in the future?
* How is life specifically better in the future because I'm living in Alignment as a Reflector?

12.
YOUR AUTHORITY

What do you think about when you hear the word 'authority'? It's probably an external force – parents, teachers, bosses, the government – in other words, someone who makes rules you have to follow.

Now, crumple up that idea of authority and toss it in the bin. It's time to meet your own inner Authority and seek out its wisdom for your life instead.

Human Design can help you redefine what authority means to you. Working with your Design prompts you to look inwards and follow your own guidance instead of looking to others for guidance and validation. To decondition from relying on external authority figures to tell you what is correct for you, and recondition yourself to trust your own internal guidance system that knows better than anyone else what is best for you.

When we talk about Authority in Human Design, we're talking about the internal compass that leads you to say 'no' to the things that don't help you thrive, and 'yes' to the choices that are aligned with who you are at your core, supporting you in the life you're here to live.

AUTHORITY 101

Your Authority guides you to be in Alignment with your most authentic self. It exists to navigate you on the best possible path for you – the path your soul has come to tread in this life. It will lead you to express your gifts, to call in people, places and experiences that serve you, and to make choices and decisions that get you to your heart's desire and purpose.

Each Authority provides guidance for decision-making based on your unique Design and energetic superpowers. Understanding your Authority will empower you to make the correct choices for you, especially when you feel you should do something differently to make others happy instead of choosing what is best for you.

REVIEW THE CENTRES

If you want to refresh your memory about the Human Design Centres, flip back to the Human Design Chart section on page 41.

Your Authority is rooted in the way your energy Centres function within your body, because Human Design teaches us to make the best decisions with the body, not the mind. Authority is not about thinking, reasoning or analysing, it's about feeling.

INNER VERSUS OUTER AUTHORITY

Learning to trust your Inner Authority is a journey from the mind into the body. In Human Design, we sometimes call the mind the Outer Authority - meaning that we do our thinking to serve others, not ourselves. All of our mental work, reasoning, analysis and learning can guide us to serve others through our gifts, talents and superpowers. But when it comes to making decisions for our own lives and well-being, we need to home in on what the body is telling us through biofeedback, intuition, our senses, our energy, our emotions and our own voices - *not* by thinking our way to the answer.

The most important thing to understand about Authority now is that while the mind is invested in your fear, identity and personality, your Authority is invested in leading you step-by-step towards living out your purpose.

One of the biggest challenges that people face when beginning their Human Design experiment is thinking they can't feel their Authority.

Let me relieve the pressure of that right now: you *can* feel your Authority. In fact, you're already working with it and have been all your life – you're just not accessing its greatest potential. What you are *not feeling* is your body. The good news is that your Human Design experiment is a process of reconnecting to the body and giving yourself full permission to listen to its wisdom.

One of the primary principles of Human Design is to move from the mind, specifically the conditioned mind, into the body for guidance and decision-making. Understanding your Authority teaches you specifically what to listen to and how to hear it so you know what is correct for you. Your body is giving you feedback all the time; it might be subtle in the beginning, but it is there.

Remember when you were a kid and just knew what you wanted and trusted your intuition? Your imagination was wild and free and somehow it came to life in weird and unexpected ways? *That* was your Authority. Unfortunately we're taught not to trust our gut, intuition and knowing as we grow up; we're told that we must analyse and think long and hard before we act. But that's all B S. Through working with your Authority, you can and will rediscover the wild freedom you thought was lost to childhood, and all that knowing is going to help you tune back into your most authentic self.

At first, practise listening to your Authority in situations that feel fun, low pressure and unimportant, for example, what to eat for dinner or what book to read. When it comes to these low-stakes decisions, the mind is less likely to get involved or critique the decisions you make, or interrupt what you're feeling in your body. Without the mind's involvement, you can notice the feelings, emotions and knowing that accompany the decision you're making and recognise that that's your Authority.

DISCOVER YOUR AUTHORITY

Pull up your Human Design bodygraph. (If you don't have one yet, you can get yours at emmadunwoody.com now.)

Underneath the full-colour bodygraph image, you'll see your name, followed by your Human Design Type. Just a few lines down on that same column, you'll find your Inner Authority.

Once you've finished reading this introduction to Authority, go through this chapter until you find the section on *your* Authority, where you'll find more details about leaning into your Authority.

For me, finding Human Design was like finding the last piece of the puzzle I had been looking for all my life.

I spent my twenties in and out of depression and suffering with my mental health. At age 35 I was finally diagnosed as having bipolar II disorder and I started to embark on a healing journey.

The biggest part of that journey was delving into who I was. I had identified myself with all the emotional issues I'd lived with for so long, I had no idea who I might be without them. I had very little help from the medical profession except for medications, and I realised I needed to investigate which path I should take on my own.

When Human Design came into my life, I felt I finally had a literal map, which laid bare the journey I had been on and confirmed that I was in fact moving into Alignment with who I felt like I really was. I could see the emotional wounding had always been meant to be part of my journey. I could also see how my Manifestor energy type, and my Emotional Authority and the emotional waves expressed themselves as bipolar symptoms. I could finally confirm that I wasn't a broken, damaged human, but someone who had been expressing my true Design all along, just not at its highest vibrations. I came to peace with my diagnosis and I now see it as the gift it actually always has been.

- Helen Anne

THE SEVEN AUTHORITIES OF HUMAN DESIGN

Emotional Authority

You are most aligned to your Design when you give yourself time to gain emotional clarity when making decisions. Sleep on it; tell people you'll come back to them later with an answer.

EMOTIONAL VERSUS NON-EMOTIONAL AUTHORITIES

People with a defined Solar Plexus in their Human Design chart are considered Emotional Authorities, and those without definition in the Solar Plexus are Non-Emotional. That means all the other Authority categories (Sacral, Splenic, Mental Projector, Self-Directed and No Inner Authority) are classified as Non-Emotional.

That said, Emotional Authority is actually the most common Authority - about 47 per cent of people on the planet have

Emotional Authority, which means that one out of two people you come into contact with will experience the world the way you do. However, it also means that about half the people you encounter in life will experience the world and make decisions very differently to you. A huge gift of Human Design and a significant part of your journey is learning to accept that everyone's path is different and valid.

Sacral Authority

You need to listen to your body's natural *Yes, I have energy for this* and *No, I don't have energy for this* instincts. This knowing comes from the gut, and it knows what is and isn't correct for you in every moment.

Splenic Authority

This Authority can be subtle, especially to begin with; it manifests as a spontaneous, immediate sense of knowing that shows up in the moment. Unlike the Sacral, the Spleen is a one-time knowing, so the more you act on it in the moment, the louder it gets.

Ego Authority

Your most authentic decisions come from what your heart desires. You see the world from the perspective of *I*: *I want, I feel, the effect on me is* … It can be misunderstood as selfish, but it's really about being empowered to do what will have the most impact.

Self-Directed Authority

You're Designed to move towards a sense of love in all of your decisions. This Authority helps you to talk out your options and bounce off another person so you can hear which direction will lead you towards more love.

Mental Projector Authority

Your Authority manifests as a knowing that drops in when you allow your natural 'thinking' side to step back. You make your most aligned decisions when you talk through what's on your mind out loud to someone who will listen and hold space.

No Inner Authority

This rare Authority, which may also be referred to as Lunar Authority, only shows up in Reflector Types. You are Designed to sample life; you make decisions by giving yourself time to get to know how opportunities, people and places make you feel before settling on a decision. Waiting 28 days, in synch with the lunar cycle, is the ideal time to give yourself when making big decisions.

Throughout each Authority section in the following pages, you'll have the opportunity to reflect and experiment with the knowledge presented. At the end of each Authority section, you'll find a series of journal prompts to help you integrate what you've learned, reflect on how your Authority has already been at work in your life up until now and plan for the future with your Authority in mind.

CHAPTER INVITATION

Once you've skipped ahead and explored your own Authority, I encourage you to come back and read through every section in this chapter. Taking the time to get to know all seven Authorities, not just your own, can have huge benefits.

First, it gives you a working knowledge of Human Design as a system. You'll have a better understanding of how your Authority works, what sets you apart from other Authorities and what you have in common with them, too.

Second, representatives of each Authority will be present in your life somewhere – whether that's at work, in your family or among your friends. Taking the time to understand every Authority will improve the relationships with the people you love – and the people you don't. Each Authority section even includes some recommendations on supporting the people in your life who were Designed to operate with that Authority.

Finally, even though you're Designed with a specific Authority, that doesn't mean you won't find information that resonates with you in other sections, beyond your own Authority. I encourage you to come to each Authority with curiosity and openness to what you can learn about yourself, as well as others.

13.
EMOTIONAL AUTHORITY MADE SIMPLE

Your most aligned decisions are made when you give yourself time to gain emotional clarity.

You have Emotional Authority if you have a defined Solar Plexus.

About half the global population operate from Emotional Authority.

THREE THINGS TO KNOW

- Heightened, in-the-moment emotions can obscure what's right for you.
- Taking time to reflect on and understand your emotions can help you gain the clarity you need.
- Total emotional clarity doesn't exist – but deeper awareness of your emotional experiences over time will help you make more aligned decisions.

THREE THINGS TO DO

- Give yourself more time than you think you need to make decisions – and let people know you will come back to them with an answer later.
- Get to know how emotional clarity feels in your body.
- Focus on consistency over 100 per cent clarity.

WHAT IS EMOTIONAL AUTHORITY?

Having Emotional Authority means that your most aligned decisions are made through tuning into your emotions and getting clarity about how you really feel – and how you *want* to feel – before moving forward.

In the following pages, we're going to:

- Unpack what it means to have Sacral Authority.
- Start experimenting with this element of your Design.
- Explore how you can best support the Sacral Authorities in your life.

FIND YOUR AUTHORITY ON YOUR HUMAN DESIGN CHART

When you generate your chart online, your Authority will be listed out for you. But you can also see it for yourself when you look at the elements of your bodygraph: if the Solar Plexus

Centre is coloured in, that means it's defined and that you have an Emotional Authority.

Emotional Authority is identifiable by a defined Solar Plexus. The Solar Plexus is the Centre that concerns our emotions – those waves of feeling that exist beyond thought, often felt viscerally in the body and the gut. Because this Centre is defined for you, your emotions play a big part in how you live. Our emotions are always switched on and flowing – from the lows of shame, guilt and apathy to the highs of love, joy and peace.

If you are Generation X or older (born in 1980 or before), then you've mostly likely been taught not to show your emotions and learned to repress them early in life. If you are Millennial/Gen Y or younger (born after 1980), then you might have had parents who rebelled against this repression of emotions and encouraged you to lean into your feelings with no restraint, and now you find you overindulge in your emotions and feel you can't control them.

This repression and/or indulgence presents a challenge, because you were Designed to feel your way through life, to experience and honour the highs and lows, the wisdom and the fear your emotions have to offer, not ignore them. As an emotional being, you are here to learn how to feel emotions without being overwhelmed or controlled by them.

Reconditioning your Emotional Authority means learning to recognise the messages your feelings are offering you. Learning to see the patterns in the ups and downs of your emotions as important signposts for what is right for your life will help you make positive changes in big and small ways.

Learning to feel comfortable taking your time and re-teaching others that you need time to respond with a decision can feel daunting at first. While it may be easier to react from whatever emotion is playing the lead in the moment, this will ultimately keep you trapped in your conditioned, homogenised life.

You are not your thoughts, you are the thinker of them. You are not your emotions, you are the feeler of them. Be witness to your emotions, allow them to be felt, but do not allow them to make decisions for you.

TAKE YOUR TIME

The single most important piece of advice that anyone with an Emotional Authority needs to take on board is this: always take more time and space than you think you need to make a decision.

Up until now, you might have let your emotions rule you, instead of giving yourself time and space to discover what is true for you underneath your emotions. Time pressure obscures what you really need, because your mind rushes you to act immediately on whatever emotion is playing the lead at that moment. However, if you give yourself the time and space to wait out the ups and downs, you'll be able to feel what's really true for you and make a clear, aligned decision on any issue that you come across.

Emotional Authority can be tiring with all those emotional ups and downs. Emotional beings tend to work in spurts of energy and then need time to recover from their emotional highs and lows. You need to prioritise rest, plain and simple.

Not only can sleep help restore your energy levels, it also gives the time and distance you need to make your most aligned decisions. When making decisions, note how you feel when you're first presented with your choices. Then sleep on it and check back in with yourself in the morning. Do you still feel the same way? If yes, you can probably safely go in the direction you're feeling drawn to. If not, you probably need even more time to reach emotional clarity about what feels correct for you.

Note that taking your time isn't necessarily about waiting for the emotion you're feeling to pass so that you can make a more 'rational' decision – it's about investing in understanding what you're really feeling, what that feeling is telling you and how your emotional responses are serving as guides for living authentically.

FEEL YOUR FEELINGS

Now that you've taken that time and space you need to gain clarity, you can use that to grow a deeper awareness of your emotional landscape.

As emotional beings, we're often misled to believe that the outer environment and the things that happen there govern how we feel (i.e. the idea that negative, dark, inhospitable environments create negative emotions). However, the opposite is true for emotional beings: you bring your emotion to whatever is happening in your outer environment, and those emotions become a filter through which you experience that environment. For example, if you're in a high emotion in the 'dark' environment, then you'll be the one who lifts everyone back up. Meanwhile, if you're at an emotional low, you could be the one who brings everyone down.

Practise becoming aware of how you're feeling. Get to know your emotional highs, middles and lows – what stories do you tell yourself and others as you move through different emotional experiences? Acknowledge how you feel and then get curious. Ask yourself: 'Do I really feel this way, or am I in a high or low emotional state?'

Think of every emotional response – fun and not so fun – as an opportunity to align to your Design more deeply. The more you learn to sit with your emotions as the witness of them – without judgement, criticism or the need to change them – the more you'll experience emotional clarity, peace and Alignment.

TRY THIS: FEEL YOUR EMOTIONS IN THE BODY

Emotional Authorities are often conditioned to intellectualise their emotional response, but doing that puts up an unhelpful wall. Instead, it's important to see the emotions as an opportunity to ground yourself in your body and get beyond what you've been conditioned to do in your mind.

A body-scanning exercise can help you get out of your head and become more aware of how you're feeling emotionally and physically. All you need to do is close your eyes and put your attention in your feet, then slowly move your attention upwards, noticing where you feel tense or loose, comfortable or uncomfortable, heavy or light, pain or pleasure throughout the body. How does that correspond with how you're feeling emotionally, or what does it reveal to you about your emotional state?

This exercise is great in circumstances where you feel overwhelmed by an emotion, but also in moments when you're not sure how you're feeling at all. Use it regularly to help you connect with your body and gain awareness of what emotions are present with you.

DON'T WAIT FOR 100 PER CENT CLARITY

One mistake that many people with an Emotional Authority make is waiting to take any decision until they feel 100 per cent sure. The truth is that all of our emotions are always in motion, they ebb and flow constantly and waiting for complete stillness will only frustrate you.

Instead of chasing 100 per cent clarity, focus on consistency. Pay attention to what consistently feels most correct for you over time (remember, you benefit from giving yourself time and space to reflect on what your emotions are telling you). If over a 24-hour period you check in with yourself several times and still feel relatively strongly that something is correct for you, then you have a green light on your decision. If you're wavering, or your emotional reaction to the possibilities is inconsistent, you might need more time, or it may not be right for you. Trust that you will know the correct thing when it crosses your path.

SUPPORTING FRIENDS, FAMILY AND COLLEAGUES WITH EMOTIONAL AUTHORITY

If you're reading this because you want to better support someone in your life who has an Emotional Authority, commit right now to giving them more space and time to make decisions. They may not realise they need that time or space, or they may not feel comfortable asking for it, so your encouragement can go a long way.

If you're a non-emotional being, your life and relationships will change for the better when you let go of frustration and annoyance at people who seem indecisive and wishy-washy in their decision-making process. They're probably Emotional Authorities and never have the clarity you enjoy. Instead, trust that their process is correct for them. By not pressuring them for an answer, you will help them find more clarity over time.

JOURNAL PROMPTS FOR EMBRACING YOUR EMOTIONAL AUTHORITY

Use these prompts to explore how your Emotional Authority feels for you.

Uncovering and healing the past:

- How in the past have I experienced challenges and not worked with my Emotional Authority?
- What decision-making behaviours need to be let go of so I can step into the power of my Emotional Authority?
- Where in my past have I been in Alignment with my Emotional Authority?

Aligning with the now:

- What resonates with me about my Emotional Authority?
- What am I resisting about my Emotional Authority?
- What am I most curious to experiment with first regarding my Emotional Authority?

Creating the future:

- What three things am I going to do today to be more in Alignment with my Emotional Authority?
- How does my Emotional Authority support my future self?
- How is life specifically better in the future because I'm making decisions from my Emotional Authority?

14.
SACRAL AUTHORITY MADE SIMPLE

Your most aligned decisions come from trusting your gut response to something in your external environment.

You have a Sacral Authority if you have a defined Sacral Centre and an undefined Solar Plexus.

About 34 per cent of the global population operate from Sacral Authority.

THREE THINGS TO KNOW

- Your Sacral Centre identifies what you *do* and *don't* have the energy for in any given moment.
- Your Sacral Response is a 'yes' or 'no' to something in your external environment.
- Your Sacral energy is all about what lights you up and what doesn't.

THREE THINGS TO DO

- Practise your Sacral Response with small and easy decisions first, like what you want to eat for dinner.
- Be curious about what lights you up. When you find it, follow it.
- Set boundaries and stop saying 'yes' when you mean 'no'.

WHAT IS SACRAL AUTHORITY?

Having Sacral Authority means that your most aligned decisions are made when you follow what lights you up and honour the immediate yes/no response to your external environment.

In the following pages, we're going to:

- Unpack what it means to have Sacral Authority.
- Start experimenting with this element of your Design.
- Explore how you can best support the Sacral Authorities in your life.

FIND YOUR AUTHORITY ON YOUR HUMAN DESIGN CHART

When you generate your chart online, your Authority will be listed out for you. But you can also see it for yourself when looking at the elements of your bodygraph: if the Solar Plexus is undefined (not coloured in) and the Sacral Centre is defined (coloured in), then you have a Sacral Authority.

Sacral Authority is identifiable by the combination of an undefined Solar Plexus and a defined Sacral Centre. The Sacral is the Centre where your gut response comes from. Since this Centre is defined in you, it's crucial to learn how to recognise, listen to and honour the immediate gut response of *Yes, I have energy for this* or *No, I do not have energy for this.*

If you have Sacral Authority, it's very possible that you've been conditioned to disconnect from your gut instincts. To believe that your immediate response is unreliable, uninformed or invalid. If you've been taught to override your initial gut instincts in favour of overthinking, you might often experience confusion and lack confidence in your decisions.

Reconditioning to embrace your Sacral Authority means first getting to know your Sacral Response. And once you learn to hear, feel and listen to the 'yes' or 'no' your gut is giving you in each moment, you can practise taking that response seriously. Choosing to trust your gut is ultimately going to result in more confidence and a more authentic sense of self, giving you more energy to follow opportunities that are in Alignment with who you really are and what you are Designed to do.

DOES ANY OF THIS SOUND FAMILIAR?

If you read the Type and Strategy sections on Generators (page 87) and/or Manifesting Generators (page 98) earlier in this book, you'll already be somewhat familiar with how the Sacral operates, and you may have already tried some of the tips and exercises recommended. I invite you to see this section as an opportunity to continue your experiment – try the exercises

again and reflect on how your awareness of your Sacral Response
has grown and changed since you began your Human Design
journey.

LEARN TO RECOGNISE YOUR RESPONSES

When you have Sacral Authority, your most aligned decisions
are made when you recognise the 'yes' or 'no' response you feel in
your gut whenever you're faced with a choice. It's essential to
listen to these gut responses , because they're giving you important information – not permission, but data. A Sacral 'yes' tells
you that you have enough energy to follow through on something. A Sacral 'no' tells you that you do not have the energy for
something – sometimes this will be because you have already
got a lot to do, other times it will be because it's just not a correct
or aligned thing for you to do.

In some rare cases, your Sacral Authority may offer up a
'maybe': when this happens, your Sacral is communicating that
this is not the correct time to act. Take a break and wait for
another opportunity to respond – the Sacral is either waiting for
divine timing or more information.

The key to understanding and harnessing the power of your
Sacral Authority lies in trusting your 'yes' or 'no' and acting on it
without overriding the decision by overthinking or judging
yourself. Start by acknowledging your initial gut response – the
felt experience of 'yes' or 'no'. This response manifests as a

feeling in the body – not just a verbal response – about what is correct for you.

PRACTISE RECOGNISING YOUR SACRAL 'YES' AND 'NO'

If you want to make aligned decisions as a Sacral Authority, you need to be able to recognise what your gut-level green lights and red lights are. These cues from your Sacral Centre manifest as a simple, immediate 'uh-huh, yes' or 'uh-uh, no' response. To get a feel for what that gut-level 'uh-huh' or 'uh-uh' feels like for you, ask a loved one to help you establish a baseline by asking you some of the following questions and inviting you to answer on the spot with a simple 'uh-huh' or 'uh-uh' response.

(If you practised this exercise earlier in the book, there's no harm in doing it again to really get familiar with what your Sacral Responses feel like, but if you're ready to go deeper, move on to the final stage of this exercise to practise making decisions from the Sacral.)

Is your name [blank]?

Were you born on [blank]?

Do you live in [blank]?

Did you have coffee this morning?

Are you hungry?

Pay attention to how your body feels when you respond with 'uh-huhs' and 'uh-uhs' to each question. As you get familiar with your 'uh-huh' and 'uh-uh' response, you can move on to bigger questions, such as . . .

Do I feel lit up by my work?

Am I satisfied with my life?

Am I working towards the things I want?

And finally, you can start to tap into your Sacral Response to make in-the-moment decisions, such as . . .

Do I have energy to do this task right now?

Do I want to participate in this activity right now?

Am I honouring my Human Design in this moment?

Practise the exercise above, and take time to journal about your experience of tuning into your Sacral Response in order to get know how your Sacral feels. Take note of patterns around how your body feels when your Sacral Response indicates a 'no' versus a 'yes'. Pay attention to how the body feels when your mind is telling you what to do versus when you're listening to your Sacral Centre, and pay attention to how your body feels when you honour your Sacral Response versus when you ignore it.

The Sacral Centre communicates through distinct physical sensations. Pay attention to the sensations associated with each response – a feeling of expansion may indicate a resonant 'yes', while a contraction in the body may signify a clear 'no'. By becoming attuned to these bodily cues, you can establish a reliable connection with your Sacral Authority, gaining clarity and confidence in your decision-making process.

The key is not to think about it – instead, allow yourself to freely respond to life.

ANCHOR YOURSELF IN THE PRESENT

The Sacral is an in-the-now response. It's incredibly powerful, but it can be missed because it moves fast. If you don't learn to recognise the response feeling when you're having it, then your mind is going to swoop in, question what you're feeling and revert back to your conditioned decision-making process. That's a problem for you, because your most aligned decisions don't come from thinking things through – in fact, overthinking keeps you from living your best life. That's why, as a Sacral Authority, it's crucial that you learn how to be present in the moment, so that you can feel the guidance your gut offers you before it's gone and your mind takes over. When this happens, don't panic. You may have missed your Sacral Response the first time around, but another opportunity will arise, giving you another chance to follow your Sacral towards what lights you up.

If you're concerned that you can't feel your Sacral Response, here are a few things you can do to bring yourself into the present moment so that you can receive the Sacral guidance you need to act in Alignment:

- Listen to and meet your body's physical needs first. Do you need to eat, sleep, use the toilet or scratch an itch? If you're ignoring these physical prompts, then you're most likely ignoring the Sacral Response as well.

- Another simple exercise is to stand in front of the cupboard or fridge and decide what you want to eat by responding to what you see. Become conscious of how it feels to respond to life from the Sacral and not the mind.
- Do something that lights you up (more on that next).

DO WHAT LIGHTS YOU UP

Sacral beings are often conditioned from birth to believe that value lies in what you can do for others, that worth is tied to how much you can get done and how well you do it compared to others. This begins at school and then spills out into all areas of adult life.

However, your true worth lies in your being the person you are, your energy, your soul and your purpose. Human Design teaches that the simple act of being you is the most valuable and worthy thing. It's not about how much you can do, it's about how you bring your unique authenticity to the world. As a Sacral being, you have a powerful source of energy and are capable of so much. The challenge is that when you get stuck spending that energy on things you think you should do – the things you merely feel obligated to do – you're more likely to burn out and less likely to make a real impact where it counts.

Obligation disconnects you from the powerhouse of the Sacral because you're not responding from what lights you up. The secret to abundant success for you is to focus on doing more of what you love, as often as you can.

This is true for every area of your life. If working in a certain industry lights you up, pursue career options that focus there. If spending the first ten minutes of your morning cuddling with your dog lights you up, do that, too. If creating social media content is fun and engaging for you, do it. If not, consider out-sourcing it to someone else, or looking for another way to promote your skills and services that is fun and engaging for you. If travelling lights you up, do that. If staying home is what excites you, that's fine, too!

But don't confuse the things that light you up with the things that are easy. Doing what lights you up may require a big investment of your energy – you'll know if the payoff is worth it when you learn to tune into your Sacral Response and get clear on what you *do* and *don't* have the energy for.

TRY THIS: HONOUR YOUR ENERGY

Spend the next week noticing your Sacral Response to every opportunity or request that comes your way in your work and personal life. With every opportunity or request, notice: *Is this a Sacral 'yes' or 'no'? Did I feel a pull forward or a leaning back in my body? Did my head nod or shake?* Look for the instant body feedback and act on it.

Journal about what happens when you honour your Sacral Response by saying 'yes' to the things you want to do, and 'no' to the things that are not correct for you. If you find yourself caught up in accepting opportunities that feel more like obligations or 'should dos', journal about how those obligations affect you.

SUPPORTING FRIENDS, FAMILY AND COLLEAGUES WITH SACRAL AUTHORITY

If you're reading this because you want to better support some-one in your life who has a Sacral Authority, commit right now to believing them when they tell you 'yes' and when they tell you 'no'. Accept these statements as full sentences. Try not to demand explanations or rationalisation; instead focus on hon-ouring the trust between the two of you.

To best encourage someone with Sacral Authority, ask them yes/no questions. Open-ended questions will confuse the Sacral.

Also make an effort to pay attention to the moments when your person seems at their most energetic and happy – encourage them to engage more fully with the things that light them up, and offer them regular opportunities to do the things they love with you by their side.

JOURNAL PROMPTS FOR EMBRACING YOUR SACRAL AUTHORITY

Use these prompts to uncover what's unconsciously holding you back, to align to your authenticity and unlock your potential.

Uncovering and healing the past:

* How in the past have I experienced challenges and not worked with my Sacral Authority?

- What decision-making behaviours need to be let go of so I can step into the power of my Sacral Authority?
- Where in my past have I been in Alignment with my Sacral Authority?

Aligning with the now:

- What resonates with me about my Sacral Authority?
- What am I resisting about my Sacral Authority?
- What am I most curious to experiment with first regarding my Sacral Authority?

Creating the future:

- What three things am I going to do today to be more in Alignment with my Sacral Authority?
- How does my Sacral Authority support my future self?
- How is life specifically better in the future because I'm making decisions from my Sacral Authority?

15.
SPLENIC AUTHORITY MADE SIMPLE

Your most aligned decisions are made when you honour your spontaneous intuitive awareness.

You have Splenic Authority if you have a defined Spleen Centre and undefined Solar Plexus and Sacral Centres.

About 11 per cent of the global population operate from Splenic Authority.

THREE THINGS TO KNOW

- The Spleen is spontaneous and in the now; if you don't listen to the wisdom when it comes, you may not get it again.
- Your intuition begins as a whisper and the more you act on it, the louder it gets.

- When your Spleen has a message for you, you will have a specific feeling in your body.

THREE THINGS TO DO

- Journal and keep a record of how your Spleen guides you.
- Act on your intuitive awareness.
- Do not allow the mind to question or discredit your knowing.

WHAT IS SPLENIC AUTHORITY?

Having Splenic Authority means that your most aligned decisions are made from your intuition – a sense of inner knowing.

In the following pages, we're going to:

- Unpack what it means to have Splenic Authority.
- Start experimenting with this element of your Design.
- Explore how you can best support the people with Splenic Authority in your life.

FIND YOUR AUTHORITY ON YOUR HUMAN DESIGN CHART

When you generate your chart online, your authority will be listed out for you. But you can also see it for yourself when looking at the elements of your bodygraph: if the Solar Plexus and the Sacral are both undefined (not coloured in) and the Spleen Centre is defined (coloured in), then you have a Splenic Authority.

Splenic Authority is identifiable by the combination of an undefined Solar Plexus and Sacral Centre, plus a defined Spleen Centre. The Spleen is the intuitive Centre, and it sends you nudges or pings, often unprompted, about what's correct for you. Having Splenic Authority is all about learning to recognise and honour the intuitive nudges that the Spleen sends your way, because it paves the path for living in Alignment.

People with Splenic Authority have usually been conditioned to ignore the intuitive nudges that they're meant to follow. Because the intuitive messages the Spleen sends often come without an external trigger, they may not appear to make sense and can be easy to dismiss as nonsense. Splenic signals can also be very subtle, especially in the beginning, so you may not even realise you're ignoring them at all.

When you're ready to recondition and step into the power your Splenic Authority has to offer, you'll need to start practising patience, discipline and self-trust. You'll need all of these if you're going to experiment with taking Imperfect Action to follow your intuition instead of casting it aside for more 'sensible' ways of navigating your life. When you give yourself permission to lean into the sometimes uncanny sense of what's correct for you that emerges from your Spleen Centre, the bounds of your wisdom and strength will come into their own and drive you towards the life you're Designed to live.

SACRAL VERSUS SPLENIC

It's easy to confuse Sacral and Splenic Authority, because many people struggle to understand the difference between gut instinct and intuition.

One of the main factors that sets Sacral and Splenic experiences apart is that Sacral Authority responds to something in your external environment, while the Splenic Authority is an internal, intuitive hit. The Sacral Response is triggered by external cues, and the Sacral 'yes' or 'no' is a direct response to a question or choice posed. The Splenic's intuitive hit, on the other hand, comes from within. You can't trigger your Splenic Authority. You have to wait for it to direct you on its own time.

TRUST YOUR SURVIVAL INSTINCTS

Having Splenic Authority is all about honouring your deep-seated survival instincts, even if you can't explain them. In the same way that birds know exactly when it's time to fly south for the winter and turtles know how to return to their birthplace to lay their own eggs, you're Designed to listen to the ancient survival signals your body is giving you.

Think of your Spleen as an intuitive radar, alerting you to what you need to do in order to survive in whatever conditions you find yourself in. Messages from your Splenic Authority manifest a little differently for everyone. Some people with Splenic Authority describe their intuitive nudges as a sudden, immediate *knowing*. For other people, it's a sensory experience – you might hear, see, know, taste, smell or feel something when the Spleen wants to nudge you in the direction of what will help you survive and thrive.

It might take time to learn to recognise, trust and act on your intuitive pings. If you feel like your intuition never speaks to you, or that you don't know how to feel it when it does, don't beat yourself up. Many people with Splenic Authority are conditioned to ignore the precious intuitive hits that the Splenic Centre sends your way, so a big part of stepping into Alignment with your Design will be about reconnecting with your intuition and allowing it to speak to you, loud and proud.

Right now, your intuition might be operating at the level of a very gentle whisper. Your job is to listen for it and to act upon the guidance your Spleen offers. Over time, your intuition will be loud and certain and give you bolder, more regular signals to help you make decisions in Alignment with your Human Design.

If you have Splenic Authority, you're really in your element when recognising and responding to your basic needs becomes second nature. This is because your Splenic Centre is concerned with your survival. So when you proactively do the work of creating well-being, safety, security and stability for yourself (by doing things like making sure you have enough food to eat, that you get quality sleep and that your body feels healthy and at ease), then your Splenic Centre will pay attention to what's beyond your immediate physical survival and start to guide you to thrive in other areas of your live.

So, practise meeting your physical needs with healthy habits before your body has to ask you to. Eat nourishing food throughout the day, exercise regularly and moderately and get a good night's sleep. Also seek out the physical affection and pleasure that you need. Your Spleen will tell you what is best for you in all these areas.

STOP QUESTIONING YOURSELF

You're Designed to trust the sudden, sometimes inexplicable intuitive hits that the Spleen delivers to you. Because you've been conditioned all your life to question those hits, you're probably not comfortable trusting those messages.

To step into Alignment with your Human Design Authority, you have to be willing to let go of everything you've been taught to think about what 'good' decision-making looks like and take the leap into trusting your own instincts, especially when you can't explain or justify them.

The moment you stop questioning the Splenic messages you're receiving is the moment your experiment with your Design truly begins.

KEEP A JOURNAL

Record every moment when you feel a strong, instinctual pull to do something. Putting these experiences in writing makes them real; it validates the experience you're having. Even more importantly, journalling about your growing awareness of your Splenic Authority will help you to recondition yourself, away from overthinking and back into your body.

Every time you feel your Spleen sending you a message – no matter how quiet, no matter how random – write it down and describe it. Focus on how you feel in your body in those moments, on what sensory experiences you're having and what you're being guided to do. Don't judge or try to rationalise the message, just put your experience down on paper.

End each journal entry with an affirmation. Something along the lines of: *This message was meant to help me survive and thrive. I trust it, and I trust myself to act on it.*

The more you practise this task, the more 'normal' working with your Authority will start to feel.

FOLLOW THROUGH

So far, in getting to know your Splenic Authority, you've practised learning to recognise it, made an effort to create a secure environment so your Authority can communicate to you with greater scope and begun the experiment of trusting those communications.

Now it's time to show your Authority that you really mean business: the ultimate way to create safety, prove trust and build a deeper and more connected bond with your Splenic Authority is to act on the guidance you're given.

When you receive an intuitive nudge, follow through on it. If you feel the strong urge to start a project, to go somewhere, to call a certain friend, to eat, to cancel a plan or whatever else – as long as it's not causing harm to you or others – just do it. Don't question it, don't postpone the action until it's convenient, just put your focus where your Authority is and follow through.

You can start small with things to help build your confidence – follow low-stakes nudges like which direction to go on a walk, or what and when to eat. Once you're confident trusting yourself with the small things, then big things like ending a relationship, buying a house or moving to another country will be easy because your mind and body will know it's safe to trust your intuition.

The more you do it, the easier it becomes. That's partially because you'll have created a habit and also because you've given your brain the evidence that trusting your intuition is safe and that following through is the hands-down best way to honour your Authority. And when you listen and act on your intuition, it will speak to you more often and more clearly. The more often and more clearly your Authority is speaking to you, the more opportunities you'll have to step into Alignment with your Design.

REMINDER: IMPERFECT ACTION BEATS A PERFECT SCORE

Even people with years of practice and lots of experience of what it's like to live in Alignment with their Splenic Authority miss a signal from time to time, so don't beat yourself up when it happens to you.

Remember, transforming your life through Human Design means taking Imperfect Action all the time. Do what you *can*, not what you think qualifies as perfect. If you're consistently following the guidance in this section, you're taking Imperfect Action and moving towards Alignment, even if you have an off day and miss the message your intuition was trying to send you.

So, instead of ruminating on moments when you miss out on an intuitive hit, simply jot the experience down in your journal and move on. The best thing you can do is be kind to yourself, make yourself feel safe enough to be imperfect and keep yourself open to the next hit.

SUPPORTING FRIENDS, FAMILY AND COLLEAGUES WITH SPLENIC AUTHORITY

If you're reading this because you want to better support someone in your life who has a Splenic Authority, focus on helping them trust their intuitive nudges, no matter how odd they might seem. That means allowing them to express themselves without demanding a logical explanation, and believing them when they tell you what they need, even if it sounds strange or random to you.

You can also help them by trusting their spontaneous nature. If they direct you to do something, trust it. When they want something specific to eat, or to take care of their physical body and well-being, encourage them to follow it. Their well-being will be influencing yours, they are guided to be well and thrive – trust it.

JOURNAL PROMPTS FOR EMBRACING YOUR SPLENIC AUTHORITY

Use these prompts to uncover what's unconsciously holding you back, to align to your authenticity and unlock your potential.

Uncovering and healing the past:

- How in the past have I experienced challenges and not worked with my Splenic Authority?
- What decision-making behaviours need to be let go of so I can step into the power of my Splenic Authority?
- Where in my past have I been in Alignment with my Splenic Authority?

Aligning with the now:

- What resonates with me about my Splenic Authority?
- What am I resisting about my Splenic Authority?
- What am I most curious to experiment with first regarding my Splenic Authority?

Creating the future:

- What three things am I going to do today to be more in Alignment with my Splenic Authority?
- How does my Splenic Authority support my future self?
- How is life specifically better in the future because I'm making decisions from my Splenic Authority?

16.
EGO AUTHORITY MADE SIMPLE

Your most aligned decisions come when you give voice to your most authentic, heartfelt desires.

You have Ego Authority if your Solar Plexus, Sacral and Splenic Centres are undefined, while your Will (also known as Ego or Heart) Centre is defined.

Only about 1 per cent of the global population operate from Ego Authority.

THREE THINGS TO KNOW

- You're Designed to be self-focused when making decisions, and that's perfectly fine!
- Making the most of your Ego Authority means listening to your heart.
- Ego energy is about desire, not emotion.

THREE THINGS TO DO

- Stop forcing yourself to do the things you really don't want to do.
- Focus on speaking from the heart and trusting what comes out.
- When making any decision, get clear on what the benefit is for you.

WHAT IS EGO AUTHORITY?

Having Ego Authority means that your most aligned decisions are made when you follow your heartfelt desires and focus on how things impact you directly. In the following pages, we're going to:

- Unpack what it means to have Ego Authority.
- Start experimenting with this element of your Design.
- Explore how you can best support the Ego Authorities in your life.

FIND YOUR AUTHORITY ON YOUR HUMAN DESIGN CHART

When you generate your chart online, your Authority will be listed out for you. But you can also see it for yourself when looking at the elements of your bodygraph: if the Solar Plexus, Sacral

and Splenic are all undefined (not coloured in) and the Will
Centre is defined (coloured in), then you have an Ego Authority.

Ego Authority is identifiable by the combination of undefined
Solar Plexus, Sacral and Splenic Centres, plus a defined Will
Centre, also known as the Heart or Ego Centre. The Will is the
Centre that deals in your heart's deepest desires – it helps you
uncover what really matters to you. Having Ego Authority is all
about giving yourself permission to prioritise your desires,
so that you can act in Alignment with what you really want out
of life.

If you have Ego Authority, you've probably been conditioned into feeling a lot of guilt and shame. Because living in
Alignment with your Ego Authority means putting your
desires first, you may have been shamed into seeing your natural mode of decision-making as selfish or short-sighted. This
couldn't be further from the truth. In reality, when someone
with Ego Authority is allowed to explore and understand what
any given opportunity has to offer them, and how it aligns
with their desires, they can harness that knowledge to make
positive and impactful contributions to their own life, and to
the wider community. What is best for you will also serve
those around you.

If you want to recondition and start making decisions from
your Ego Authority, you'll need to be brave enough to unapologetically speak out loud what you want and need. When you
release the shame of 'selfishness' and replace it with a sense of
self-worth, you'll finally be free to make choices in line with

your authentic self and create the life you were Designed – and deserve – to lead.

BE SELFISH

The first step towards living in Alignment with your Ego Authority in Human Design is to embrace the selfishness that you've been conditioned to hide away. The truth is, putting yourself first is not only acceptable but crucial for your well-being. You're Designed to be guided by your 'selfish' interests, and when you allow that to be true, you'll be able to accomplish so much more – for yourself, but also for other people.

We live in a world that's uncomfortable with people who know what they want and go after it. But the people who judge you for your desires first are the real selfish ones – their judgement of you keeps you and them from the positive outcomes that arrive as a result of your self-direction. So don't let guilt or external expectations suppress your true self. Instead, consider selfishness as a means to honour your desires, operate from a place of authenticity and bring your best self to the rest of the world so that everyone wins.

Choosing to view selfishness in a positive light can be a powerful lesson in self-love and acceptance. Despite societal stigmas, understanding that selfishness can be constructive enables you to build a foundation of self-respect and confidence. By unapologetically acknowledging and prioritising your needs and desires, you unleash your full potential and radiate authenticity, fostering more harmonious interactions with the world around you. Embrace your authentic nature, honour your desires and watch as it transforms your life for the better.

TRY THIS: REFRAME SELFISHNESS

Get out your journal and cast your mind back to a time when you felt you acted 'selfishly'. Reflect on that experience and ask yourself:

What desire fuelled my actions?

What was the outcome of my actions?

How did my actions benefit me?

How did my actions benefit others?

Did I experience shame or pride in my actions?

What did this experience teach me?

Now reflect on a time where you wanted to act in your own best interest but ultimately didn't because you felt too ashamed or self-conscious of being seen as 'selfish'. Reflect on that experience and ask yourself:

What 'selfish' action did I want to take?

What conditioned action did I take instead?

What happened right before my fear of being seen as 'selfish' was triggered?

What desire did I suppress by not acting 'selfishly'?

How would things have turned out better if I'd honoured my own desires?

What did I, and my community, miss out on because I suppressed my desire?

KNOW - AND DECLARE - WHAT YOU WANT

If you have an Ego Authority, the most important thing you can do for yourself when making decisions is to get clear about what decisions will benefit you. You can do this through a process of soundboarding, where you talk about your desires, about your options and feelings until you come to a place of clarity about what you want and feel comfortable acting on that.

A sounding board is a person who will listen without an agenda or a desire to fix you or your problem. They listen and repeat back what they hear you say and not say, the tone you use and maybe ask you further questions for you to talk through so that you can come to a heartfelt knowing of what is correct for you.

This process can take time, and you may want to talk about the same topic a number of times with the same person, with different people or even talk about it out loud to yourself or a favourite pet. It's the process of hearing yourself speak and iden-tify your desires out loud that matters.

USE YOUR WILLPOWER WISELY

The Ego Centre is where your willpower lives, so as someone with Ego Authority, you have impressive reserves of will. It's an incredible gift, but one you may have been conditioned to misuse as a way of forcing yourself through tasks and experi-ences that don't feel correct for you.

To step into Alignment with your Ego Authority, you have to let go of the idea that you need to will yourself through anything and everything. Instead, refocus your willpower on accomplishing your true desires – the things that you have abundant creative juice for – and let go of the conditioned need to force your way to success.

Think of your willpower like a savings account: when you put money in – or in this case rest and recover to create more energy – then you'll have savings there when you need them. However, if you keep spending all your energy and willpower by forcing yourself through life, then you will end up empty, with no energy for anything.

When you reallocate your willpower away from things that you don't want, and towards things that you do, you'll have even more access to your own will. Think of acting in your own interest as a cheat code for getting more access to your superpowers.

TRY THIS: A WEEK OF WANT

Spend a week doing what you want, the way you want to.

That doesn't necessarily mean ditching all your projects because you don't want to work, though. Instead, it means giving yourself permission to prioritise the tasks and projects that are most heart-filling and beneficial to you.

Start by re-evaluating your to-do list. Instead of organising it by what's most urgent, organise it by what brings in the most benefits to you - listen to what your heart is telling you when it comes to identifying what those benefits might be. (This will take some thought, so set aside some proper time to think about it.)

Then, live out your week by focusing on doing what benefits you the most. If you feel uninspired by or resentful of your work, try to revitalise yourself by reminding yourself of the benefits. If you can't name any benefits for a task, ditch it or delegate it!

At the end of the week, journal about your experience. Record what worked, what didn't and how your relationship to meeting your own desires has changed since you began this experiment.

Make sure you plan rest and recovery time to get your energy back in the bank.

SUPPORTING FRIENDS, FAMILY AND COLLEAGUES WITH EGO AUTHORITY

If you're reading this because you want to better support someone in your life who has an Ego Authority, the most important thing you can do for them is champion and celebrate the desires they express to you. Respond with enthusiasm and comment on how you see that acting on this desire benefits them and others. This teaches them that you're a safe person to share their heart with; it tells them that you're on their team and that you see their value.

But be careful not to give advice or directives – your loved one or colleague needs you to offer a sounding board, not a permission slip. They need to be allowed to focus on their own desires, not try to play the right cards to appeal to yours. So even when something they want to do doesn't directly benefit you, try to see how it benefits them in their life and celebrate their decision to follow their desire.

And most of all, let go of any judgements you may hold of their self-focused process. Know that this is the way they move through life; it's how they're Designed to see the world and make sense of it. When their actions appear selfish, trust that this is all part of the process. In time, you will see how their decisions serve everyone else too.

JOURNAL PROMPTS FOR EMBRACING YOUR EGO AUTHORITY

Use these prompts to uncover what's unconsciously holding you back, to align to your authenticity and unlock your potential:

Uncovering and healing the past:

- How in the past have I experienced challenges and not worked with my Ego Authority?
- What decision-making behaviours need to be let go of so I can step into the power of my Ego Authority?
- Where in my past have I been in Alignment with my Ego Authority?

Aligning with the now:

- What resonates with me about my Ego Authority?
- What am I resisting about my Ego Authority?

- What am I most curious to experiment with first regarding my Ego Authority?

Creating the future:

- What three things am I going to do today to be more in Alignment with my Ego Authority?
- How does my Ego Authority support my future self?
- How is life specifically better in the future because I'm making decisions from my Ego Authority?

17.
SELF-DIRECTED AUTHORITY MADE SIMPLE

Your most aligned decisions come when you head in whatever direction will result in loving action from you, and loving encouragement from others.

You have Self-Directed Authority if you have a defined G Centre that is connected to the throat, and undefined Solar Plexus, Sacral, Spleen and Will Centres.

Between 2 and 3 per cent of the global population operate from Self-Directed Authority.

THREE THINGS TO KNOW

- It's important you hear the tone, words and intonation of your words, as this will help you to know your correct direction.

- The advice you have for other people is often the advice you need to take yourself.
- Your decisions are about going in the correct direction to experience more love.

THREE THINGS TO DO

- Find a sounding board who will listen, hold space and allow your voice to be heard clearly by you.
- Stop asking for advice when really you just need to talk it out to hear your own advice.
- Let yourself have as many conversations as it takes to come to clarity.

WHAT IS SELF-DIRECTED AUTHORITY?

Having Self-Directed Authority means that your most aligned decisions are made when you're listening for the correct direction for you, often to experience more love. Put simply, you need your friends and loved ones to act as sounding boards so that you can hear yourself process what you're feeling and make a decision out loud.

In the following pages, we're going to:

- Unpack what it means to have Self-Directed Authority.
- Start experimenting with this element of your Design.
- Explore how you can best support the Self-Directed Authorities in your life.

FIND YOUR AUTHORITY ON YOUR HUMAN
DESIGN CHART

When you generate your chart online, your authority will be
listed out for you. But you can also see it for yourself when looking at the elements of your bodygraph: if the Solar Plexus, Sacral,
Splenic and Will are all undefined (not coloured in) and the G
Centre is both defined (coloured in) and connected to the throat,
then you have a Self-Directed Authority.

Self-Directed Authority is identifiable by the combination of
undefined Solar Plexus, Sacral, Splenic and Will Centres,
plus a defined G Centre that is connected to the throat. The
G Centre is where your sense of higher self identity and
unconditional love lives. Having Self-Directed Authority
means that your journey to Alignment is twofold: you need
to learn to hear your own voice and trust the direction
it's sending you in *and* you need to find the people who
understand that loving you means listening to you without
agenda.

If you have Self-Directed Authority, you may have been
conditioned to listen to other people's opinions about what you
should do more than your own sense of what direction is correct
for you.

You may often question your own choices and default to
following others' lead any time you're faced with a decision –
that's because as a Self-Directed Authority, you naturally take in
and amplify other people's energy and choices, which can

confuse you when it comes to feeling out what you really need to do for yourself.

To reclaim clarity and confidence when making decisions for yourself, you need to take time to talk out what you're feeling about a topic or decision. As you speak through your feelings to a trusted sounding board, you'll feel into what is correct for you and ultimately articulate it – trust that you'll know it when you hear it come out of your mouth.

Your journey to Alignment means claiming your Self-Directed Authority by learning to hear and trust the power of your own voice, trusting your innate direction and being led by the desire to experience more love.

Reconditioning and owning your Self-Directed Authority means learning to respect your own voice first and foremost, and teaching the people in your life to give you the space and comfort you need to speak your truth. When you surrender your need for other people's approval and learn to prioritise your own sense of the correct direction for you, you'll be able to make more aligned, powerful decisions and move towards the destiny you were Designed for.

STOP ASKING FOR ADVICE

If you have Self-Directed Authority, you thrive when you talk out your problems and work through your decision-making process out loud with the encouragement of someone else. This can sometimes be challenging, because you're also influenced by other people's energy – that means that when you invite people into conversations about what you should do, you probably end up giving them more influence over your decisions than is correct for you.

However, when you constantly ask for advice, you're essentially outsourcing your decision-making power to someone else. You're denying your Self-Directed Authority to do its job by asking someone else to do the heavy lifting for you, even though the only person qualified to make correct decisions for you is *you*.

Here's the thing: you don't need advice. You need a supportive ear. And there's a difference. One tells you what to do. The other holds space for you to figure out what you're going to do on your own terms.

So, the next time you have a decision to make and feel tempted to seek out advice, play with other ways of holding space for your own voice, like recording a voice note to yourself, or talking out your problems with a pet – this can scratch the itch of hearing yourself think, and guarantees you won't get any advice!

And if you find yourself really in need of a human ear, call up a friend and use this script: 'There's something on my mind and I'm struggling to work through it alone. I don't want any advice, but would you be willing to let me tell you about it so that I can hear myself think?'

LISTEN TO YOUR OWN VOICE

The secret to living in Alignment with your Self-Directed Authority is in the name – you need to direct yourself. You're Designed to follow your own direction, so you need to get comfortable being honest with yourself about what you want and what direction you want to go in.

Now is the time to commit to following your own truth, your direction and authenticity, instead of giving your power away to others to make those decisions for you.

Once you stop seeking out advice that leads you away from your own inner wisdom, you can start listening for what's true to you and following your own advice.

TRY THIS: THINK OUT LOUD

In the last section, you picked up a few new tricks for seeking out your own advice (like talking to a pet or recording voice notes to yourself), but it's also helpful to invite your voice out to play even if you don't have a specific issue that you need to think out loud about.

To get comfortable hearing and listening to your own voice, consider narrating your everyday thoughts and actions to yourself as they come. This is a technique that many teachers suggest to people learning a new language, because it helps speakers get comfortable and recognise their new language as a commonplace part of their lives.

The same is true for learning to hear your authentic voice - the more you use it in run-of-the-mill situations, like explaining out loud to yourself what you're doing, what you think and why, the easier it will be to access your inner wisdom and direct yourself when you need to make a decision.

MODEL UNCONDITIONAL LOVE FOR YOURSELF

Having Self-Directed Authority is all about cultivating a deep respect for your own innate sense of what's correct for you, giving your inner voice the opportunity and safety to express itself, and ultimately following your own direction.

To create a strong foundation for your journey to Alignment with your Authority, you need to focus first on reconditioning your relationship with being loved.

Because you have a defined G Centre, feeling loved for who you are is hugely important to you. It's a crucial motivator for your actions, and it's a powerful source of energy for you. The problem is that your societal and cultural conditioning may have cut you off from the most powerful source of motivating love there is: self-love.

Many people with Self-Directed Authority have been conditioned away from their inner wisdom and made to believe that love is an external gift that has to be bestowed on them by someone else. That couldn't be further from the truth: experiencing love starts within you, and you don't need anyone else's approval or participation to access the power of love in your life.

If you want to rediscover your inner voice and step into Alignment with your Self-Directed Authority so that you can consistently make decisions that honour your Human Design and lead you towards the life you were meant to live, you have to start by offering yourself the love you deserve, and removing the power you've given other people to determine your level of lovability. You are infinitely lovable, but the only person who can prove that to you *is* you.

TRY THIS: AFFIRM YOURSELF

This exercise will help you do two important things: hear your own voice and experience your own unconditional love for yourself.

The first step is to craft an affirmation - or series of affirmations - that express your love for yourself. Your affirmation can be as broad or specific as you like. You might start with something like: *I love myself no matter what,* or you might go into detail and affirm a specific element of your life or being, like: *I love the way I use my artistic talent to express myself* or *I love the way I keep my children fed and safe.*

Repeat this mantra to yourself at least once every day, but ideally as often each day as possible. Say it out loud, several times in a row, taking a deep breath and breathing it into your cells with every repetition - really listen to your voice as you express love for yourself.

Craft more affirmations as time goes on and keep listening to your own voice as you show yourself love.

SUPPORTING FRIENDS, FAMILY AND COLLEAGUES WITH SELF-DIRECTED AUTHORITY

If you're reading this because you want to better help someone in your life who has a Self-Directed Authority, the absolute best thing you can do for them is refrain from offering advice. Instead, let them know that you're available to be a sounding board to let them work out their own thoughts.

In practice, this means focusing way less on telling your loved ones what you think they should do, or even sharing your own experiences in similar situations, and instead keeping the conversation focused on them and their experiences.

Ask them questions like:

- How do you feel about being faced with this issue?
- Can you talk me through the options you have?
- What challenges do you anticipate if you go with one option over the other?
- What's most important to you in this situation?
- What advice would you give me if I came to you with this issue?

JOURNAL PROMPTS FOR EMBRACING YOUR SELF-DIRECTED AUTHORITY

Use these prompts to uncover what's unconsciously holding you back, to align to your authenticity and unlock your potential.

Uncovering and healing the past:

- How in the past have I experienced challenges and not worked with my Self-Directed Authority?
- What decision-making behaviours need to be let go of so I can step into the power of my Self-Directed Authority?

- Where in my past have I been in Alignment with my Self-Directed Authority?

Aligning with the now:

- What resonates with me about my Self-Directed Authority?
- What am I resisting about my Self-Directed Authority?
- What am I most curious to experiment with first regarding my Self-Directed Authority?

Creating the future:

- What three things am I going to do today to be more in Alignment with my Self-Directed Authority?
- How does my Self-Directed Authority support my future self?
- How is life specifically better in the future because I'm making decisions from my Self-Directed Authority?

18.
MENTAL PROJECTOR AUTHORITY MADE SIMPLE

Your most aligned decisions come when you get out of your own head and trust your intuitive knowing to show you the way.

You have Mental Projector Authority if you have a defined Ajna Centre that is connected to the head and/or throat, and if all the Centres below your throat are undefined.

About 3–4 per cent of the global population operate from Mental Projector Authority.

THREE THINGS TO KNOW

- You can't make a truly aligned decision if you're stuck inside your head.
- You don't have to create a perfectly rational, ten-point plan for every decision you make.
- Journalling can be a life-changing tool for you.

THREE THINGS TO DO

- Process your thoughts out loud or on paper.
- Experiment with letting go of your need to think things through.
- Let your friends and loved ones know that you need their ears, not their opinions.

WHAT IS MENTAL PROJECTOR AUTHORITY?

Having Mental Projector Authority means that your most aligned decisions are made when you get out of your own head and make space for your intuition. You do this when you think out loud to another person who is listening and holding space for you. Getting your thoughts out of your brain and declaring them out loud or on paper helps you hear what is correct for you and what action to take. In the process of thinking through your decision out loud and asking yourself questions, your intuition will have the opportunity to offer you a clear answer about what to do, and when you hear it, you'll *know*.

In the following pages, we're going to:

- Unpack what it means to have Mental Projector Authority.
- Start experimenting with this element of your Design.
- Explore how you can best support the Mental Projector Authorities in your life.

FIND YOUR AUTHORITY ON YOUR HUMAN
DESIGN CHART

When you generate your chart online, your Authority will be listed out for you. But you can also see it for yourself when looking at the elements of your bodygraph: if the Solar Plexus, Sacral, Splenic, Will and G Centres are all undefined (not coloured in) and the Ajna Centre is defined (coloured in), then you have a Mental Projector Authority.

Mental Projector Authority is identifiable when all of the Centres below the throat are undefined, and when the Ajna Centre is defined and connected to the head and/or throat. The Ajna Centre is where all of your thoughts and opinions form. It's the Centre of mental processing. Having Mental Projector Authority means learning to honour your thought process without getting trapped in your own mind.

If you have Mental Projector Authority, you may have been conditioned to lean too heavily on your reasoning skills to guide you. Reason and logic are incredible tools; however, we're often conditioned to prioritise them over our intuitive sense, and over how we feel in our body. When you develop that habit, your decision-making process becomes incomplete – you're only listening to your mind, not your whole self. Your journey to Alignment means learning to think in ways that invite your intuitive sense of what's correct for you to provide clarity, instead of getting lost in a thought loop so that your intuition can't find a gap in which to connect with you.

To recondition and work effectively with your Mental Projector Authority means focusing on creating ways of getting out of your own head and thinking, making room for your intuition to come through. When you start to see your thought process as a tool for inviting your intuition to the table, you'll learn to recognise cues from your intuition sooner, feel a clearer sense of connection between your mind, body and spirit and be able to step into the full power of your Design.

GET YOUR THOUGHTS OUT OF YOUR HEAD

Mental Projectors often struggle with getting stuck inside their own heads. The experience can lead to overthinking, decision paralysis and mistrusting your own intuition.

Mental Projectors *are* great thinkers. You've got a talent for recognising patterns, developing well thought out and structured plans and sniffing out all of the nuance and detail of every situation. These are incredible gifts, make no mistake. They're particularly useful if you've been invited to help someone in your life work through their own journey to make a decision: you can help them identify troublesome patterns, build out thoughtful plans and attend to the finer details, all while they tap into the inner wisdom their own Authority provides.

The challenge is that your expert thinking skills can keep you stuck in a perpetual thinking loop that will never get you to a correct decision. The truth is that you're not Designed to make decisions based on thinking alone – it's only when you learn to let go of the sense of control that thinking gives you, and listen to your intuition instead, that you'll be empowered to discover what decisions are correct for you.

It's not that you need to abandon your thought process altogether, but that you need to go beyond it. One of the simplest and most effective ways to do that is to relieve your mind of the pressure by getting your thoughts out of your head. Commit them to paper or record an audio or visual diary. Seek out friends who are great listeners and will respect your thought process, rather than those who jump straight into offering advice.

Once you get into the practice of channelling your thoughts into something tangible, like a recording or a notebook or even a conversation, it can get you out of your mind and free you up to receive messages from other parts of yourself – namely, the sense of knowing, rather than thinking, that comes from your Ajna Centre.

RELEASE THINKING AND EMBRACE KNOWING

When you relieve yourself from the pressure to rigorously think through every decision you make, you create room for a different kind of intelligence to come through: your intuition.

By Design, people with Mental Projector Authority experience a powerful, intuitive sense of knowing when something correct drops into their mind. The problem is that you've often been conditioned to disregard that intuitive feeling in favour of your rational thinking process. *Or* you've learned to credit your critical thinking as the ultimate source of your knowing, which delays and distracts you from the real truth: that your 'illogical', inexplicable intuition is the secret ingredient for your success. You waste valuable time and energy trying to rationalise and justify what you already know, instead of taking your natural intuition seriously in the first place.

For you, stepping into Alignment means embracing your 'irrational' side as much as you've idolised and leaned on your critical reasoning. It means learning to trust yourself, and finding freedom in the fact that you don't need to *think* your way to a solution. Instead, you can tune in to the innate knowledge you already have and make decisions that match up with your powerful, intuitive Authority.

TRY THIS: RECORD THE DIFFERENCE BETWEEN THINKING AND KNOWING

Use your journal as a sounding board to identify the difference between what you think and what you know.

For the next week, every time you have a decision to make, start by drawing a vertical line in your journal to create two columns. Label one 'What I think' and the other 'What I know'. Give yourself space to record your experiences in both columns.

Under 'What I think' might be the patterns, expected outcomes and considerations your mind calls your attention to in regards to the decision you're making.

In the 'What I know' column, record your instinctive reactions to your options.

Ask yourself:

- How do the different choices I have make me feel in my body?

- If there were no consequences to consider, which option would I immediately go for?

- What feels correct for me, despite the considerations I feel pressure to take time to think about?

Commit to choosing in favour of what you *know* versus what you *think* as many times as possible over the next week, and record the outcome. Ask yourself:

- How did it feel to trust my intuition?

- What patterns emerged when I started trusting my intuition?

ASK FOR THE SUPPORT YOU NEED

Because you need to get out of your head and make space for yourself to hear and embrace your intuitive wisdom, it can be really helpful to have a few go-to people in your life who are comfortable listening to you process your experiences and decisions out loud.

Asking others to help you while you explore can be a challenge for people with Mental Projector Authority, since you're so used to relying on what happens inside your own mind to guide you. And it might initially feel like a step backwards; you might find yourself asking, 'Why would I need someone else's support if the point is to learn to trust my own intuition?'

The truth is, having a good listener on speed dial will help you work through your thoughts and hear what you know. Because you thrive when you release your thoughts from your head by getting them down on paper and speaking them out loud, having an audience as you work through a decision will force you to get out of your head and start to clear a way for accessing your intuitive sense of knowing.

But that doesn't mean that you should just jump in and invite anyone and everyone to act as a sounding board for you. Choose friends, family or colleagues who are willing to listen and can hold back from giving advice. You need to surround yourself with people who are patient and attentive, not bossy or judgemental.

When you find those people, be clear with what you need from them, namely: their ears only. Ask them to listen and to ask open-ended questions that centre your process, not their opinions. Prepare them for the possibility that you'll probably need to talk through your thoughts and feelings several times before it all comes clear.

TRY THIS: MAKE A SOUNDING BOARD JOB DESCRIPTION

In your journal, draft a list of criteria that make someone a good sounding board. Feel free to let your thinking side rule this part of the task. Reflect the behaviour patterns that make up good (and bad) listening skills, look back at your past experiences of talking out problems with other people and identify what worked and what didn't. Review what you know about your Authority (as well as your Type and Strategy) to help you put together a list of qualities that make up the kind of person who would make a good sounding board.

Once you've done that, ask yourself: 'Who in my life would, or already does, make a good sounding board for me?' and allow your intuition to answer. Write down the name of the first person who comes to mind and give them a call. Ask them to listen to you tell them what you've learned about your Authority, and hold space for you to explore what that means for you going forward.

SUPPORTING FRIENDS, FAMILY AND COLLEAGUES WITH MENTAL PROJECTOR AUTHORITY

If you're reading this because you want to better support someone in your life who has a Mental Projector Authority, the best thing you can do for them is encourage them to get out of their own heads. Gift them with journalling supplies, vlogging or podcast equipment. Or give them the gift of your time and attention – encourage them to call you more, or leave you voice notes about what's going on with them. When they do call or leave messages, positively reinforce that behaviour by always thanking them for sharing.

You can also help those with Mental Projector Authority in your life by being selective with the questions you ask them.

Keep things open-ended and focus on helping them move further out of their head and deeper into their intuition. Ask questions like:

- What feels correct for you?
- What is your intuition telling you?
- How would you like this situation to turn out?
- How do the different options available make you feel in your body?
- What do you already know to be true?

JOURNAL PROMPTS FOR EMBRACING YOUR MENTAL PROJECTOR AUTHORITY

Use these prompts to uncover what's unconsciously holding you back, to align to your authenticity and unlock your potential.

Uncovering and healing the past:

- How in the past have I experienced challenges and not worked with my Mental Projector Authority?
- What decision-making behaviours need to be let go of so I can step into the power of my Mental Projector Authority?
- Where in my past have I been in Alignment with my Mental Projector Authority?

Aligning with the now:

- What resonates with me about my Mental Projector Authority?
- What am I resisting about my Mental Projector Authority?
- What am I most curious to experiment with first regarding my Mental Projector Authority?

Creating the future:

- What three things am I going to do today to be more in Alignment with my Mental Projector Authority?
- How does my Mental Projector Authority support my future self?
- How is life specifically better in the future because I'm making decisions from my Mental Projector Authority?

19.
NO INNER AUTHORITY MADE SIMPLE

Your most aligned decisions come when you take your time and consciously put yourself in environments that make you feel held and energised.

You have No Inner Authority when none of the Centres in your chart are defined.

About 1 per cent of the global population operate from No Inner Authority.

THREE THINGS TO KNOW

- The people and environments you engage with have a powerful effect on your energy.
- You're Designed to flow from one thing to another, to follow where the energy takes you.
- You need time to know what's correct for you.

THREE THINGS TO DO

- Do an audit of how the people and places in your life feel; if it's not a good feeling, then it may be time to move on.
- Use the lunar cycle as a structure for tracking your energy.
- Record your experiences with the people, places and things you engage with to help you identify what's correct for you.

WHAT IS NO INNER AUTHORITY?

Having No Inner Authority means that you are not guided by a consistent internal sense of what's correct for you, because your energy moves and changes with your environment and the people around you. You're Designed to read the energy of your environment and the people you surround yourself with as a barometer to help you make aligned decisions. You'll need lots of time (we're talking several weeks, whenever possible) to observe, reflect and come to the conclusion that's correct for you.

In the following pages, we're going to:

- Unpack what it means to have No Inner Authority.
- Start experimenting with this element of your Design.
- Explore how you can best support those with No Inner Authority in your life.

FIND YOUR AUTHORITY ON YOUR HUMAN
DESIGN CHART

When you generate your chart online, your Authority will be
listed out for you. But you can also see it for yourself when looking at the elements of your bodygraph: if none of the Centres on
your chart are defined (coloured in), then you have No Inner
Authority.

No Inner Authority is identifiable when none of the Centres of
the body are defined on your chart. When this is the case, it
means you don't source your consistent energy from within the
body, but absorb and reflect the energy you come in contact
with, based on who you're with and where you're at. This isn't a
bad thing – it means you have a whole world of energy to draw
on; you just need to learn to discern what energy you take in
and reflect back to the world.

If you have No Inner Authority, you may have been conditioned to see your natural way of decision-making as a liability:
people may have told you you're too impressionable, or that
you're wishy-washy. As a result, you might have pushed yourself
in the opposite direction, forcing yourself to make decisions
quickly and resolutely, and sticking stubbornly with them even
when they don't feel right for you. But you were Designed to
take your time, to feel deeply and to seek out positive influences
and environments that can help you recognise what's right for
you – to sample life and make decisions by giving yourself time

to get to know how opportunities, people and places make you feel before settling on a pathway.

Your journey to Alignment means accepting your unique way of being in the world, allowing yourself to flow from one energy to the next and trusting that, when you surround yourself with people and things that empower you, your path will become clear.

To recondition and embrace the fact that you have No Inner Authority, you need to focus on putting yourself in places and around people whose energy makes you feel good. You'll also need to practise taking plenty of time before you come to any firm conclusions, and learn to release yourself from any expectations to be decisive. You were Designed to feel your way, slowly but surely, towards a life that is aligned with who you are, and when you finally give yourself permission to make decisions in your own time, based on your own observations and sense of security in your environment and relationships, you'll be one step closer to the life you were born to live.

TAKE YOUR DECISION-MAKING PROCESS SLOWLY

When you have No Inner Authority, you need to be free to take as long as you need to come to decisions that are correct for you. When you take your time, it allows you to reflect on what you need as you move through different environments and interact with different people. This helps you to be sure the decisions you're making are true to you, not just reactions to the energy you've most recently been in contact with.

You should always take as much time as you need, and where you can, you should experiment with giving yourself a full lunar cycle to make big decisions.

In some Human Design circles, having No Inner Authority is also referred to as Lunar Authority, in large part because the moon can be such a helpful regulating tool for people operating from this Authority. The moon, with its ever-changing yet consistent phases, can become a reliable external guide to help you navigate life's choices more effectively.

By synching your decision-making with the lunar cycle, you establish a connection to external rhythms that complement your unique Design. This external reference point not only bolsters your decision-making by slowing your process down, it also helps you create a more harmonious relationship with the natural flow of life. The consistent cycle of the moon becomes a reliable compass, offering a framework for your choices based on the energetic shifts happening each month within you. Embracing this approach allows you to navigate decisions in a way that respects your individual Design and acknowledges the cosmic influences that surround you.

TRY THIS: KEEP A MOON JOURNAL

Starting at the next new moon, journal daily over the course of 28 days, tracking your energy as the moon moves through each new phase.

Ask yourself these five questions:

- How do I feel today?

- How does my feeling correspond to the current phase of the moon?

- Where, with whom and on what have I spent my energy today?

- What feels true for me today?

- Is what felt true for me yesterday still true today?

At the end of the 28-day period, reflect on your journalling experience. Ask yourself:

- What truths persevered and what truths fell by the wayside as I moved through the moon's cycle?

- What people, places and things consistently made me feel good, and what people, places and things tended to make me feel bad?

- During which phase of the moon did I feel particularly clear-headed about what is correct for me?

Once you feel confident about keeping track of your energy as it moves through the lunar cycle, you can graduate to studying how the moon moves through the specific makeup of your Human Design chart.

TAP INTO THE ENERGY AROUND YOU

Without a set internal compass, being mindful of how you feel in your surroundings is crucial for making decisions that align with your authentic self.

To start, pay attention to how different places and people influence your mood. Recognising when you feel off in a particular spot or around specific individuals is key. This mindfulness enables you to choose environments that provide a positive boost to your energy levels – more on this later.

When you have No Inner Authority, it's really important to incorporate practices such as meditation or grounding exercises into your routine. These activities can help you establish a connection with your own energy and enhance your ability to comprehend the vibes around you. Regular self-reflection and journalling are also powerful tools for recognising patterns and discerning which environments contribute positively to your energy and which may be draining.

By tuning into the energy, you can create a supportive space for your unique Human Design to shine through in the decisions that you make.

TRY THIS: SCAN YOUR BODY AND THE ENERGY SURROUNDING YOU

This twist on a body-scan meditation is particularly powerful for people with No Inner Authority. It will help you make meaningful connections to the external energies acting on you, and understand how those energies impact you.

All you need to do is close your eyes and put your attention in your feet, then slowly move your attention upwards, noticing where you feel constricted or relaxed, comfortable or uncomfortable, heavy or light, pain or pleasure throughout the body.

Once you've guided your attention through the body, allow your awareness to reach further out. Notice what you feel and experience beyond the body by tuning into the physical environment you're in, the mood surrounding you and any other external factors you can sense. Notice how the way you feel shifts and changes from place to place and depending on the energies you're interacting with.

PUT YOURSELF IN ENVIRONMENTS THAT MAKE YOU FEEL GOOD

As someone with No Inner Authority, you are always taking in energy, amplifying it and reflecting it back. So it's absolutely crucial for you to carefully select the spaces and people you surround yourself with, since the energy of your environment can significantly impact your well-being and decision-making process.

Choosing environments that feel good or challenge you to grow creates a supportive backdrop for your life's journey. Negative or chaotic atmospheres can easily send you down the incorrect path for you, potentially leading to decisions that are not in fact yours, but rather your reflection of someone else's decisions. By deliberately opting for environments that nurture and uplift you, you can make choices that align with your authentic self and bring you closer to a life of ease and empowerment.

But there's more to cultivating an energetically supportive lifestyle than simply avoiding or seeking out pre-existing environments. You also have the power to *create* the kind of environment that encourages you. That means actively inviting people and things that make you feel good into your life; it means designing a home that energises you; and it means choosing to take action based on what you know works, not simply waiting for the right energy to arrive. By consciously curating the spaces you inhabit, you gain greater awareness of the energies that impact your decision-making, fostering an environment in which your unique Design can flourish. Put simply, the environments you choose to cultivate and create become a canvas upon which your Human Design can express itself authentically, allowing you to navigate life's decisions with a greater sense of clarity and purpose.

TRY THIS: CURATE YOUR ENVIRONMENT

Choose a space in your home that you can transform into an energetic safe haven. Fill it with things that make you feel fun, secure, happy, comforted and empowered. For example:

- Pictures of people or things that make you feel empowered.

- Textures and colours that make you feel at ease and comfortable.

- Smells and sounds you enjoy.

- Quotes that inspire and resonate with you.

- Functional items like books, toys or devices that you love spending time with.

Keep in mind that what feels good will also be ever-changing for you. Allow yourself to transform as the things, people and places that you feel good around change.

SUPPORTING FRIENDS, FAMILY AND COLLEAGUES WITH NO INNER AUTHORITY

If you're reading this because you want to better help someone in your life who has No Inner Authority, commit right now to giving them more time to make decisions. Actively let them know there's no pressure and that they deserve to take as much time as they need to choose what's correct for them.

Another thing you can do is ask them for feedback about how your energy affects them. Get curious about the things you do that empower and inspire them, and be conscious of the ways your negative interactions with them hinder them on their journey.

Make sure to ask them lots of clarifying questions about what they want and feel. Get curious, be present and hold space for them to show themselves to you over time.

JOURNAL PROMPTS FOR EMBRACING NO INNER AUTHORITY

Use these prompts to uncover what's unconsciously holding you back, to align to your authenticity and unlock your potential.

Uncovering and healing the past:

- How in the past have I experienced challenges and not worked with having No Inner Authority?
- What decision-making behaviours need to be let go of so I can step into the power of having No Inner Authority?
- Where in my past have I been in Alignment with having No Inner Authority?

Aligning with the now:

- What resonates with me about having No Inner Authority?
- What am I resisting about having No Inner Authority?
- What am I most curious to experiment with first regarding having No Inner Authority?

Creating the future:

- What three things am I going to do today to be more in Alignment with having No Inner Authority?
- How does having No Inner Authority support my future self?
- How is life specifically better in the future because I'm making decisions from having No Inner Authority?

20.
YOUR PROFILE MADE SIMPLE

Okay, beautiful human, you're deep into your Human Design experiment now, so let's check in for a brief review.

So far over the course of this book you've learned:

- How to look at your chart without getting overwhelmed.
- What your Type is, and how it brings together all the beautiful and varied elements of your chart that make you *you*.
- What your Strategy is, and how working with it can help you uncover your purpose on this planet.
- What your Authority is, and how it can guide you to make decisions that are correct for you and your unique Design.
- How to support and uplift the people in your life by understanding and honouring their Type, Strategy and Authority.

Everything you've learned so far has given you new tools for stepping more confidently into your Design and showing up in the world with a clear sense of purpose.

Now it's time to dive into Profile, an element of your chart that can help you further unlock your purpose and, crucially, put that purpose into practice.

Think of it like this: your Strategy guides you to *what* you're here to do (your purpose). Your Authority guides you on *where* to put your energy so that you can prioritise that purpose. Then your Profile illuminates *how* you can, and already do, act that purpose out in the world.

THE COSTUME OF YOUR PURPOSE

Your Profile identifies significant themes that play out in every area of your life, as well as helping you recognise how you view the world and how the world views you.

Traditional Human Design describes Profile as the 'costume of our purpose'. In films and theatre, costume is an important symbol that helps us understand what's happening. A pointy hat tells us we're dealing with a witch; another character's white coat tells us they're a doctor. These are important signifiers because they tell us what kind of story we're dealing with and what we might be able to expect.

Your Profile functions similarly – it gives you important context clues about the kind of story you're in and the active role you can navigate in that story.

You can also see your Profile as a key theme that moves with you through your life. Your Profile can tell you how you learn, what's most important to you, how you know if you're Designed to focus on yourself or others first and what the world wants *from* you.

THE 12 PROFILES OF HUMAN DESIGN

Every Profile is made up of a combination of two archetypes, or 'Lines'. In the following chapters, we'll dive into the characteristics of each of the six lines, so that you can get to know both elements of your Profile in depth.

DISCOVER YOUR PROFILE

Pull up your Human Design chart. If you don't have one yet, you can get yours at emmadunwoody.com now.

Underneath the full-colour bodygraph image, you'll see your name, followed by your Human Design Type. Just a few lines down in that same column, you'll find your Profile. It will appear as two numbers, for example, 3 / 5 or 4 / 6.

These numbers come from the columns you'll see on each side of your bodygraph. On the right, you'll see a column titled 'Personality'. The decimal point following the first whole number in the Personality column represents the first Line in your Profile. On the left, you'll see a column titled 'Design'. The decimal point following the first whole number in the Design column represents the second Line in your Profile.

Once you've finished reading this introduction to Profile, go through this chapter until you find the sections that correspond to each of your Profile Lines, where you'll find more details about leaning into each of your Profile Lines.

THE SIX PROFILE LINES

Line 1 – The Investigator: People with Line 1 in their Profile are natural learners and teachers. You activate your purpose through seeking out and sharing knowledge.

Line 2 – The Hermit: People with Line 2 in their Profile are born talents; they are here to share their natural gifts. You activate your purpose when you honour your talents.

Line 3 – The Martyr: People with Line 3 in their Profile are Designed to learn by experimentation through trial and error. You activate your purpose when you break away from convention and experiment.

Line 4 – The Opportunist: People with Line 4 in their Profile thrive in community and relationships. You activate your purpose when you're connected to and supported by other people who share your values.

Line 5 – The Heretic: People with Line 5 in their Profile are here to heal, solve and lead. You activate your purpose when you focus on healing yourself and use your experience to help others heal.

Line 6 – The Role Model: People with Line 6 in their profile grow into great sources of wisdom over time. You activate your purpose when you cultivate patience and allow yourself the time you need to learn and reflect before you share your wisdom.

PERSONAL VERSUS TRANSPERSONAL LINES

Lines 1-3 are considered 'Personal' Lines. That means these Lines prompt you to look inwards, to focus on yourself and on your journey first. From there, you share what you have discovered with the world.

Lines 4-6 are considered 'Transpersonal' Lines, and they invite you to look outwards, to notice what is happening with others and how what you see and experience triggers your journey of growth.

YOUR PROFILE IS A COMBINATION OF TWO LINES

Everyone has two Profile Lines: the first number is your Personality and the second number is your Design.

Let's break it down:

Your first number or Personality Line is your conscious experience. It reflects the things you consciously resonate with, and it will often match the way others describe you. To a large degree, your Personality Line represents who you *think* you are and the patterns of behaviour you are aware of.

Someone who has Personality Line 4, for example, will resonate with the themes of relationships, community and connection – they're aware that they value good relationships as much as food and water, whether they find themselves surrounded by good relationships already, or are in active pursuit of finding their people.

Your second number or Design Line is representative of your unconscious and your body. If your first Line is who you *think* you are, then your second Line is who you *feel* you are, and this can be more subtle and unconscious.

DOING THE MATHS

Once you've begun to explore each of your Profile Lines on their own, start doing the work of putting them together. Ask yourself:

- What aspects of my first and second Profile Lines resonate most with me?
- How do my Lines show up in everyday life?
- How have I been resisting the themes present in my Lines?

We've already touched on how each of the six Profile Lines is either 'Personal' (Lines 1–3) or 'Transpersonal' (Lines 4–6). Now that you're looking at your Profile as a whole and how your two Lines work together, you can determine if you have a 'Personal' or 'Transpersonal' Profile.

Personal Profile

You have a Personal Profile if your Profile begins with the smaller of the two numbers (i.e. 1 / 3 or 4 / 6). This means that your life's journey is about *you* first. You're here to understand yourself, and activating your purpose requires a focus on your own experiences first. It's not selfish to prioritise your experience; it's simply how you're built. Trust that when you follow this element of your Design, you'll be more poised to make an impact on others than if you tried to ignore your own experiences.

Transpersonal Profile

You have a Transpersonal Profile if your Profile begins with the bigger of the two numbers (i.e. 5 / 1 or 6 / 2). That means your journey comes via what you notice and experience with others. You learn and act most authentically based on what you see *others* experiencing or what's going on *outside* of yourself. You're Designed to notice your world and the people in it, and take action based on what's going on in your environment and community, not just what's going on in your own body or mind.

Throughout each Profile Line section in the following pages, you'll have the opportunity to reflect on and experiment with the knowledge presented. At the end of each Profile Line section, you'll find a series of journal prompts to help you integrate what you've learned, reflect on how you've already stepped into the power of your Profile and discover how you can take steps to activate your purpose with your Profile in mind.

CHAPTER INVITATION

You're probably going to want to skip ahead and read about your own Profile Lines first, and that's a wise move. But as usual I recommend that once you've explored your own Profile Line sections, you come back and read through every section in this chapter. Taking the time to get to know all six Profile Lines, not just your own, can have huge benefits.

First, it gives you a better working knowledge of Human Design as a system. You'll understand better what's unique and powerful about your gifts and what you have in common with others, as well.

Second, each Profile will be present in your life somewhere - whether that's at work, in your family or among your friends. Taking the time to understand every Profile will give you a better sense of what drives the people you love - and the people you don't.

Finally, let me remind you: no one part of your Design defines you. Your Profile is just another access point for self-knowledge that your Human Design chart supplies. I encourage you to come to each Profile with curiosity and openness to what you can learn about yourself, as well as others.

21.
LINE 1
PROFILE – INVESTIGATOR

If your Profile includes Line 1, you harbour a natural desire and ability to master knowledge. You value discovery and might hold ambitions of becoming a trusted expert who others seek to learn from and be guided by.

Learning is a theme that will follow you throughout your life – you'll always be on a journey of curiosity and discovery. Your hunger for knowledge and your dedication to finding answers is apparent to the people around you – you may not know it, but the people in your life see you as a trusted authority.

At the same time, you can get caught up in the fear that you can't act or make an impact until you've learned and mastered everything there is to know. Even though the people around you see your dedication to learning as the thing that gives you authority, you might feel that you never have enough knowledge, answers or certifications. The truth is that you will never have all the answers – that's impossible. The more important truth is that, in actuality, you will often have all the answers you need to move forward.

You're an expert *because* – not in spite – of the answers you don't have yet. Because you're fuelled by finding knowledge, you'll always be someone people can count on to help them find the answers they need.

Using your Profile to live out your purpose – and to show up in the world as your most authentic self – means flipping the script and recognising what everyone else around you already knows: your drive for answers and knowledge is your greatest strength. When you accept yourself as a lifelong learner – and recognise that you serve the planet by always being ready to investigate anything and learn more – you can shed the self-consciousness that comes with not knowing everything right away, and don the costume of your purpose by embracing your dual role as a student and a teacher.

ABOUT THE ARCHETYPE

Line 1 is associated with the Investigator archetype. While this language certainly reflects the natural curiosity and drive for knowledge that fuels people with Line 1 Profiles, it's also not the whole picture. The truth is that you search for answers because you fear the not-knowing, so you get to the bottom of things and then you build strong, sturdy foundations that create safety and stability for yourself and others.

LINE 1 FOR PERSONALITY

If you have a Line 1 for your Personality (the first number in your Profile), your relationship with learning has likely played a very obvious role in your life up to now. You're driven by creating safety and security in your life. This comes from having knowledge, with no surprises or unknowns – that's what makes you feel safe.

You may have enjoyed researching, studying and expanding your knowledge at school, and perhaps now work in a role and/or field like academia, journalism, spiritual studies or another profession that emphasises learning, such as medicine or engineering. Or you might be a lifelong hobbyist and love dipping into new skills and topics for the fun of it.

You're probably the first to say that you love to learn, and also the first to admit you're not an expert when you feel insecure about the level of knowledge you've got on a specific topic.

So how do you level up and use your established love of learning and knack for finding answers to better live out your Human Design, and feel more in tune with your purpose on this planet?

It's simple: step into your role as an expert. Offer your wisdom to others when guided to do so by your Human Design Strategy and Authority.

If someone calls you an expert or thanks you for all that you know, thank them and own that this is your superpower. Stop being afraid of what will happen if you don't know the answer.

Instead, trust that you are hardwired to find the answers you don't yet know, and that it's your natural tenacity, not the knowledge itself, that makes you valuable.

LINE 1 FOR DESIGN

If you have Line 1 for your Design number, your relationship with learning may be more subtle. You may not immediately resonate with being a 'good student' or feel that you have a natural drive to find answers. The truth is that your curiosity simply manifests differently.

Since your Design Profile Line is concerned with the body and with what lies in your unconscious, your curiosity and hunger for knowledge may be less obvious. In fact, your desire to create safety and security through knowledge may be something you don't consciously think about; however, it's something you're doing most of the time.

Because your Line 1 is on the Design side, you will need information first to feel safe. Once you have made a decision to do something, you desire the information and knowledge required to move you forward, and once you have it you will establish a safe foundation and continue to progress.

To shine a light on the Line 1 superpowers that have been hiding in your subconscious, prioritise researching knowledge and finding information on whatever you are drawn to. Know that the fear you have around not knowing enough is your intrinsic motivation to find answers, gain knowledge and become a powerful authority.

The number one block or shadow that Line 1s experience is analysis paralysis, the fear that they do not yet have or know enough, and they will not take action because of it. This is absolutely not true! You will always have more knowledge and information than you really need; it's only the fear that will tell you otherwise.

JOURNAL PROMPTS FOR UNLOCKING THE POWER OF YOUR LINE 1 PROFILE

Use these prompts to uncover what's unconsciously holding you back, to align to your authenticity and activate your purpose.

Uncovering and healing the past:

- Where in the past have I expressed the shadow of my Line 1 Profile?
- What in my past needs to be healed and let go of so I can step into my power?
- Where in my past have I been in Alignment with my Line 1 Profile?

Aligning with the now:

- What resonates with me about my Line 1 Profile?
- What am I resisting about my Line 1 Profile?
- What am I most curious to experiment with first regarding my Line 1 Profile?

Creating the future:

- What three things am I going to do today to activate my purpose through my Line 1 Profile?
- How does my Line 1 Profile support my future self?
- How will stepping into the power of my Line 1 Profile help me support others in the future?

22.
LINE 2 PROFILE – HERMIT

If Line 2 appears in your Profile, you thrive when you follow the things that you master easily, i.e. your natural talents. While that might sound like generic advice, take a look at Lines 1 and 3 and you'll see how differently you're built. Although the Lines that surround you really come into their own when they're seeking and sharing knowledge, or experimenting through experiences to discover what works and what doesn't to find what's correct for them, you're Designed to work with what you've already got. You're not here to gather knowledge and experiences first, you're here to develop your natural talents.

As a Line 2, building and maintaining *awareness of* and *confidence in* your gifts is going to be a theme you encounter throughout your life. While you possess natural talents, you may not always be aware of them, or give them the credit and respect they deserve. Embracing your Line 2 Profile is all about recognising the value of what you naturally bring to the table.

You might struggle with feelings of guilt when you choose to do what feels easy or natural for you, because you've been conditioned to believe that good, meaningful work must also always feel hard. The truth is, for you, ease is a sign that you're doing it right. The easier and more natural something feels, the more potential impact it has for you and your wider community.

ABOUT THE ARCHETYPE

Line 2 is associated with the Hermit archetype. And it's true, you master your talents when you withdraw into your own space and focus on nurturing, exploring and developing your natural talents. But don't take this label too far: being a Line 2 doesn't make you innately antisocial or require you to ostracise yourself from your loved ones and society at large. It simply reflects that you do well when you make time and space to do your own thing, on your terms.

As a Line 2, you probably don't like being told what to do and most likely are not one for listening to authority or taking unsolicited direction. Working in traditional hierarchies will be frustrating for you, because you work best doing things your own way, learning from your peers and going at your own pace.

To identify your Line 2 gifts, pay attention to what other people tell you you're good at or ask you for help with. Sometimes these things will be practical, like being a mentor, playing a sport or consulting on something you have had a lot of success with. Sometimes it will be less obvious: maybe you're often asked to bring people together or to provide comfort. These are your natural talents, too.

LINE 2 FOR PERSONALITY

If you have Line 2 for your Personality, you likely already have an idea about what your gifts are. Maybe you're a great cook, have a knack for figures and sums or have shown artistic or physical talent from a young age. Your gifts and your lifestyle are probably already somewhat intertwined.

You naturally gravitate towards doing work that you love, your way, and that allows you to lean into your gifts. And you probably bring your gifts home with you, too – your talents are not only in the workplace.

Your job now is to really own what you're good at and what feels natural for you. When someone calls out your talent, respond by giving your talent to the world. Refer back to your Strategy and Authority to know when your gifts can be used to activate your purpose. Ask yourself: *Am I bringing my talents out into the world or hiding them away?*

LINE 2 FOR DESIGN

If you have Line 2 for your Design, your journey to acknowledging your gifts may take a little more attention. Your gifts might seem subtle and harder to name. Trust that even if you can't immediately identify your gifts, they're there and already at work in your life – even if you can't articulate them just yet.

Since your Design Profile Line is concerned with the body and with what lies in your unconscious, your gifts might be less obvious and more rooted in felt experience. You might have a natural empathy that lends itself to healing and social work, or you might have stellar intuition or a close connection to nature.

To find the gifts that shine through your Design Line 2, start by cultivating a reflection practice. Look back over each day and identify what came easily to you and what other people tell you you're good at. Track the patterns over time and allow your gifts to be revealed.

The number one block or shadow that Line 2s experience is that they hide themselves away – 'they never have to risk being seen'. The truth is your talents are here to be seen and shared, and that means leaving your Hermit cave and rising to the requests to share your talents.

JOURNAL PROMPTS FOR UNLOCKING THE POWER OF YOUR LINE 2 PROFILE

Use these prompts to uncover what's unconsciously holding you back, to align to your authenticity and activate your purpose.

Uncovering and healing the past:

- Where in the past have I expressed the shadow of my Line 2 Profile?

- What in my past needs to be healed and let go of so I can step into my power?
- Where in my past have I been in Alignment with my Line 2 Profile?

Aligning with the now:

- What resonates with me about my Line 2 Profile?
- What am I resisting about my Line 2 Profile?
- What am I most curious to experiment with first regarding my Line 2 Profile?

Creating the future:

- What three things am I going to do today to activate my purpose through my Line 2 Profile?
- How does my Line 2 Profile support my future self?
- How will stepping into the power of my Line 2 Profile help me support others in the future?

23.
LINE 3 PROFILE – MARTYR

Having Line 3 in your Profile means that living out your purpose is going to require lots of experimentation, with some wins and lots of lessons. You're Designed to put yourself out there, call out what doesn't work and discover what does through experiential learning.

The ups and downs of your life's journey will turn out to be your greatest strengths, because everything you experience along the way will help you build great resilience and a sense of adventure. All the experiences you gather make you incredibly relatable to others; they feel you have walked in their shoes ... and in many cases you have.

It's important to reject the common idea that we can fail. The truth is we can't fail at anything; we're either winning or learning.

Because you are here to call out what *doesn't* work, you must experience what doesn't work and then from all your experimentation you will share what *does* work and why. Sometimes going in the wrong direction is the only way to land in the right place.

The journey to embracing your Line 3 can be challenging – it may feel unfair that you have to do everything the 'hard way'. But trust me, a fellow Line 3, when I say this: embracing your experimental path is going to make you an unstoppable force for positive change. The resilience, ingenuity and empathy that come with navigating life as a Line 3 are worthy rewards for all the twists and turns you'll face along the way.

ABOUT THE ARCHETYPE

Line 3 is associated with the Martyr archetype. This name is not empowering or useful in my opinion, so while it is common language in traditional Human Design circles, I avoid using it in most cases. While it's true that having a Line 3 Profile means, especially in the beginning of your experiment, that you may find yourself in situations where you can't help thinking *Why me?*, you have the capability to determine how you respond to that initial impulse to play the victim, and most Line 3s I know do not make martyrs of themselves. When you're empowered and view your Line 3 as a journey of adventure, you will never fall into Martyr energy. It's totally okay to wonder *Why me?*, as long as you're prepared to give yourself a resourceful answer: *Because I was Designed to learn through this experience, and one day I'll be able to help someone else navigate it because I've lived it.*

People with Line 3 profiles tend to have a strong sense of justice and truth – because you've walked through so many different experiences, you can recognise situations that cause suffering or misrepresent what you know to be true. You can lean on your own experiences and hard-won wisdom to stand up for what's right and to advocate for others.

To really step into the purpose-activating power of your Line 3 Profile, the first thing you need to do is rebrand failure in your life. Stop classifying your experiences as winning or losing, and start seeing your journey as one of winning or *learning*. Trust that you'll always find a way through, no matter the road block, and that every high and low you encounter is strengthening your ability to show up for yourself and for others.

LINE 3 FOR PERSONALITY

If you have Line 3 for your Personality, you're Designed to be a bold and confident experimenter. You actively reject societal norms. You know that you're at your best when you simply jump into whatever challenge is in front of you and mess around until a solution presents itself. You might feel at home working in roles that have freedom to try new things and experiment – environments where you can iterate and apply win-or-learn thinking. You might be drawn to unconventional things and opportunities to break and remake something, and you probably get a kick out of trying new things and going to new places.

To get the most out of what your Line 3 Personality has to offer, double down on making messes. Recognise trial and error as an essential part of your process and celebrate it. Step even more fully and unapologetically into your commitment to live an unconventional life – the lessons you'll learn will be worth the winding road.

LINE 3 FOR DESIGN

If you have Line 3 in your Design Profile, it's important to reflect on the feedback from your body as you experience and experiment with the ups and downs of your trial-and-error lifestyle.

Your Design Profile Line reflects what's going on for you on the physical and subconscious level. Paying attention to your body and listening to what it's telling you so that you can really understand and learn from your embodied experience in the world is crucial for you.

Whenever you feel unclear or not sure what you want or what is correct for you, you must have some sort of experience: you need to get out and try it out, whatever 'it' is. Through experiencing and experiment, you will become aware of what to *not* do or what to *stop* doing and what specifically needs to be done to get the best result.

You have the potential to be very resilient and adventurous when you no longer fear mistakes or what doesn't work. You see things in ways others are not open enough to see, let alone put into action – you are the explorer and adventurer in all areas and fields.

The number one block or shadow that Line 3s experience is the fear of failure or making a mistake. Instead, they quit or run away because they find it easier to start over than face failure. They can be commitment-phobic and choose the next shiny thing instead of staying committed to the thing they are Designed to break, remake and share with others.

For help identifying what feels correct for you, refer back to your Strategy and Authority.

JOURNAL PROMPTS FOR UNLOCKING THE POWER OF YOUR LINE 3 PROFILE

Use these prompts to uncover what's unconsciously holding you back, to align to your authenticity and activate your purpose.

Uncovering and healing the past:

- Where in the past have I expressed the shadow of my Line 3 Profile?
- What in my past needs to be healed and let go of so I can step into my power?
- Where in my past have I been in Alignment with my Line 3 Profile?

Aligning with the now:

- What resonates with me about my Line 3 Profile?
- What am I resisting about my Line 3 Profile?
- What am I most curious to experiment with first regarding my Line 3 Profile?

Creating the future:

- What three things am I going to do today to activate my purpose through my Line 3 Profile?
- How does my Line 3 Profile support my future self?
- How will stepping into the power of my Line 3 Profile help me support others in the future?

24.
LINE 4
PROFILE – OPPORTUNIST

If Line 4 appears in your Profile, you're very much a people person. You value community and crave meaningful relationships. You activate your purpose when you're working alongside and empowering others.

Feeling secure in, comforted by and supportive of the people you're in relationships with is a foundational part of your identity. As a result, you'll find that creating and maintaining a sense of connection and community with others is a theme that will follow you throughout your life's journey. You'll make your biggest impact when you're surrounded by people and relationships that align with your purpose – whether that's through collaborating with like-minded colleagues, being helped by loved ones who respect your values and goals or putting your skills to work to encourage and grow others.

ABOUT THE ARCHETYPE

Line 4 is associated with the Opportunist archetype. In the context of this Profile Line, that language refers to the fact that opportunity will come to Line 4s whenever they're in community with and surrounded by their people. If you're in the right place with the right people, the right thing is going to arrive. Your job is to show up for the people who you feel supported and energised by; when you do, you will be the rising tide that lifts all boats.

Having Line 4 in your Profile indicates that you're a natural-born influencer. It's important to be mindful of how and where you go about stepping into positions of influence.

The most important thing about being the influencer or the one that brings the new idea to the group for spreading is that you choose the people and groups you are a part of carefully. You might have a tendency to try and stick out bad relationships; you may notice you can be more afraid of being alone than with the incorrect people for you. However, when you spend time with people who do not value you or listen to you, your super-power of influence is lost.

As you grow and evolve, make sure to check in with yourself – do you have influence with the group you're engaged with? Do you feel safe in these relationships? If the answer is 'no', then you must choose to move on from those people and find a new group. It will feel scary, but it will completely transform your life when you find your authentic, aligned people.

To activate your purpose as a Line 4, start by focusing on how the relationships in your life are bolstering you, and just as crucially, how you're helping the people you're in relationships with. Take stock of which relationships give you energy, comfort and satisfaction, and commit to continuing to nurture these relationships. Reflect too on where your help would be most needed and appreciated. How can you step more fully into your role in the communities you're a part of?

LINE 4 FOR PERSONALITY

If you have a Line 4 Personality, you're likely confident and comfortable being a part of group projects. You might already work or volunteer in community-driven spaces where meaningful connection is a key driver of success. You might feel best in environments that bring groups together, like in a school. Maybe you feel motivated being a part of a team or mission – you're a people person, so how you feel about your work and self will often come down to the relationships you have within each area of your life. You classify yourself as a people person, and probably as an extrovert, and you make an effort to reach out to new people and explore potential friendships and connections.

You may, however, lack boundaries and overcommit or people-please to avoid rejection. It might be hard for you to say 'no' even when you really want to. And, because you're trying to be everyone's friend instead of focusing on the select few relationships where you feel most authentically you, your impact can be diluted.

However, boundaries in relationships will gain you more depth and connection, and upgrade the quality of your relationships, leaving you with the energy to look after yourself. After all, you are the most important thing in your life, not your friends, family, clients or colleagues.

To increase your impact and influence, be mindful to follow your Strategy and Authority when committing to people and projects. Consider how those commitments feel – do you feel safe and valued, or not?

All your important opportunities will come through your community, friends and relationships, so the higher the quality of your relationships, the higher the quality of your opportunities.

LINE 4 FOR DESIGN

If you have Line 4 for your second Profile number, activating your purpose through your Profile may take some extra reflection.

Since your Design Profile Line is concerned with your unconscious, you may not be as aware of relationships that are not serving you or you may fear rejection. You may also not realise what a brilliant friend and team member you can be when you're being authentic and aligned. In either case, it's important that you begin to draw what matters to you in relationships out of the unconscious and into the light.

Start by reflecting on the relationships you have in your life. Be honest with yourself – do you feel valued? Do you have influence? Do you spend more time trying to make the crappy relationships good than investing your energy in the aligned ones?

JOURNAL PROMPTS FOR UNLOCKING THE POWER OF YOUR LINE 4 PROFILE

Use these prompts to uncover what's unconsciously holding you back, to align to your authenticity and activate your purpose.

Uncovering and healing the past:

- Where in the past have I expressed the shadow of my Line 4 Profile?
- What in my past needs to be healed and let go of so I can step into my power?
- Where in my past have I been in Alignment with my Line 4 Profile?

Aligning with the now:

- What resonates with me about my Line 4 Profile?
- What am I resisting about my Line 4 Profile?
- What am I most curious to experiment with first regarding my Line 4 Profile?

Creating the future:

- What three things am I going to do today to activate my purpose through my Line 4 Profile?
- How does my Line 4 Profile support my future self?
- How will stepping into the power of my Line 4 Profile help me support others in the future?

25.
LINE 5 PROFILE – HERETIC

If Line 5 appears in your Profile, impact, healing and solutions are your greatest strength. You have a passion for service and you activate your purpose through healing wounds – your own and other people's. A natural leader, you thrive when you're holding space for others and facilitating a healthier, happier, more authentic way of being. And you're not just here to aid others on a one-to-one basis; when you really lean into your purpose, you'll find yourself making strides towards healing your community, and even the world at large, because you're here to make a big impact.

Over the course of your life, you'll explore and come to understand what it means to heal all kinds of wounds and traumas. Actively healing your own trauma and fear is a critical part of your journey. When you're in tune with your own wounds, and can recognise where and how you need care, you'll be a more effective leader, healer and guide for others on their own journey.

As a Line 5, others will likely recognise that you can help them heal – people are drawn to you like moths to a flame; they *need* your help, your solutions and guidance. But the same people who need your help may also project their own wounds onto you and accuse you of the very thing that they have been wounded by in the past. This is not you – it is their pain. Choosing not to take other people's projections personally and having compassion instead of judgement will be critical for your health, well-being and impact.

Boundaries are paramount for Line 5s or you will find yourself in constant service without support or care given back to you. It is important to understand that you are here to have great impact, and the better your boundaries, the bigger the impact you will have. Not all wounds are yours to heal and not all those who will come to you are ready to heal, so trust your Strategy and Authority when deciding where to put your powerful energy.

ABOUT THE ARCHETYPE

Line 5 is associated with the Heretic archetype - someone who speaks out, who leads others to a new way of being. This can be uncomfortable. You may fear being attacked or disliked, but your power and leadership matter. Remember, others project their own wounds onto you and blame you for things that aren't your fault. The challenge is that often you see what others cannot, and others may not see you're trying to help. It is important to wait for others to ask for your guidance and coaching. Follow your Strategy and Authority and you will be received and valued where you're needed most.

Though you're hardwired to help others, you'll need to learn how to know when you've done enough and recognise that it's time to move on. You're not here to save everyone – you're here to do what you can and empower others to take responsibility for their healing while also taking care of yourself. Do not allow yourself to take the weight of the whole world on your shoulders. Instead, trust that helping and empowering others to solve and heal what holds them back will create a snowball effect of meaningful impact that is ultimately bigger than you.

To step into the power of your Profile, put your emphasis first on your own healing journey and then allow that experience to expand out and touch the lives of others. Focus on who you can help based on your experience, Strategy and Authority. Trust that you will be guided to those you are here to serve, and never lose sight of what comfort and love you need along the way.

LINE 5 FOR PERSONALITY

If you have Line 5 as your Personality, you're probably very aware of your own passion for helping and healing and are driven to lead and have an impact. You're the kind of person who brings hot soup over to a sick friend's house, or is on speed dial anytime someone in your life takes a knock at work, in their relationships or even in their physical and mental health.

You take pride in being a good listener and you've probably pursued a career that reflects your passion for helping others heal. You might be a literal healer. You have a talent for problem-solving and solutions-based thinking alongside a desire to be with people, to help them and lift them up.

Your Line 5 Personality helps you step into your purpose because you're naturally propelled to be where you're needed. And if you're ever unsure of where your healing and solutions can make an impact, listen to your Strategy and Authority for guidance.

LINE 5 FOR DESIGN

If you have Line 5 as the second number, consider that your call to healing is rooted in the body. You might, quite literally, have healing hands – a knack for healing in all sorts of modalities.

Since your second Profile Line is concerned not only with the body but with what lies in your unconscious, you might be unaware of your journey to uncover the emotional and mental wounds you need to heal from. Trust that the more work you put into discovering and healing yourself, the more impact you'll be able to make when the time comes to help others.

With Line 5 as your second number, it is important to feel into your body and get to know how it speaks to you. Your body knows what needs to heal and what others need to heal, so learn to listen and act on its powerful messages.

JOURNAL PROMPTS FOR UNLOCKING THE POWER OF YOUR LINE 5 PROFILE

Use these prompts to uncover what's unconsciously holding you back, to align to your authenticity and activate your purpose.

Uncovering and healing the past:

- Where in the past have I expressed the shadow of my Line 5 Profile?
- What in my past needs to be healed and let go of so I can step into my power?
- Where in my past have I been in Alignment with my Line 5 Profile?

Aligning with the now:

- What resonates with me about my Line 5 Profile?
- What am I resisting about my Line 5 Profile?
- What am I most curious to experiment with first regarding my Line 5 Profile?

Creating the future:

- What three things am I going to do today to activate my purpose through my Line 5 Profile?
- How does my Line 5 Profile support my future self?
- How will stepping into the power of my Line 5 Profile help me support others in the future?

26.
LINE 6
PROFILE – ROLE MODEL

If Line 6 appears in your Profile, then you are playing a long game in life. You're not here to burn bright and fast, but rather to trust that through the process of living, learning and developing wisdom, you are naturally maturing into the exact role model the universe is going to need you to be one day.

Line 6 in your Profile indicates three specific phases that will unfold in your life:

- From 0 to 30 years of age, you'll be learning and living in a trial-and-error experience (it's worth reading up on Line 3, even if Line 3 doesn't appear in your Profile!).
- From 30 to 50, you'll withdraw into a period of self-reflection where you'll begin to really process the experience of your early life, to heal, make sense of your life so far and ultimately find wisdom.
- From 50, you'll hit a point in life where you're ready to bring all your wisdom to the world. When that happens,

the knowledge and experiences you've got to share will be deeply impactful for those who are meant to be mentored by you.

ABOUT THE ARCHETYPE

Line 6 is associated with the Role Model archetype. As you might have guessed, this indicates that you're here to lead others by example and as a mentor. Activating your purpose is all about recognising that every stage of life you navigate is an important step in crafting your ultimate vision for the world. The lessons you learn, the self-knowledge you pursue and the wisdom you share are all equally important parts of the life you live, and how others will ultimately perceive you and learn from you.

Patience is a skill that will serve you well. Without it, you may find yourself always in a hurry to get somewhere or be something you're not, when the truth is you're already being the person you need to be to become the version of you you're dreaming of becoming.

Though you'll move through distinct phases in your life, that does not mean that you have to wait until you're 50 to live your purpose. In fact the opposite is true: everything that you experience *is* your purpose.

If you're a Line 6 wondering what you can do to activate your purpose today, start by reflecting on what phase of life you're in. If you're in your trial-and-error phase, give yourself permission to go out into the world and try things out; recognise this is its own act of living out your purpose. If you're in your wisdom-gathering phase, prioritise reflection, study and self-care; trust that it is active engagement with your purpose. And as you step into the full potency of your purpose heading into your fifties, respect the experience and wisdom you're bringing to the table – it's been hard-won and it needs to be shared. This is your purpose coming into its full power.

LINE 6 FOR UNDER-FIFTIES

If you have Line 6 as your first number and you're under 50, then you may have had a number of ups and downs and learned a great deal from them all. Even before you are in full Role Model form, you will no doubt be someone others come to for advice and guidance. The work you do may be as a visionary, the big-picture thinker and the one able to see beyond current constraints like 'the way things have always been done'. You possess the imagination to see something completely 'out there' as a real possibility – like a world without money, for example.

You will feel an internal drive to realise your purpose, and often you will have to do work that feels like you are a part of something bigger, with meaning and vision, so align to the work that feels purposeful and visionary.

LINE 6 FOR PERSONALITY

If you've got a Line 6 Personality and are over 50, now's the time for you to allow others to come to you for your vision, to be wise and a strong teacher and mentor. You will be called upon to share what you know and what you see, called on to show others the way – however, make sure you have solid boundaries, because otherwise others will draw down on all your energy.

LINE 6 FOR DESIGN

If you have Line 6 as your Design Profile, you may not be fully aware of this slower but deeply unique path that you walk. The map of your future – the path that promises you wisdom as you age – may not feel like something you're consciously connected to. You might instead feel a physical itch to get on the move, a desire to be further ahead that you can feel in your bones.

Embracing Line 6 as your Design Profile means learning to slow your pace down, reminding yourself that you do have time and you don't need to achieve everything right this minute. Being present and in the moment is how you allow the higher wisdom to guide you.

JOURNAL PROMPTS FOR UNLOCKING THE POWER OF YOUR LINE 6 PROFILE

Use these prompts to uncover what's unconsciously holding you back, to align to your authenticity and activate your purpose.

Uncovering and healing the past:

- Where in the past have I expressed the shadow of my Line 6 Profile?
- What in my past needs to be healed and let go of so I can step into my power?
- Where in my past have I been in Alignment with my Line 6 Profile?

Aligning with the now:

- What resonates with me about my Line 6 Profile?
- What am I resisting about my Line 6 Profile?
- What am I most curious to experiment with first regarding my Line 6 Profile?

Creating the future:

- What three things am I going to do today to activate my purpose through my Line 6 Profile?
- How does my Line 6 Profile support my future self?
- How will stepping into the power of my Line 6 Profile help me support others in the future?

PART 3

BRINGING IT ALL TOGETHER

27.
HOW TO UNPACK YOUR CHART: A SAMPLE READING

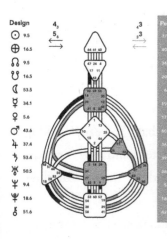

Design		Personality		Name	Emma Dunwoody
☉ 9.5	4₃ 5₆	3₃ 3₃	37.3 ☉	Type	Manifesting Generator
⊕ 16.5			40.3 ⊕	Strategy	To Respond
☊ 9.5			34.6 ☊	Inner Authority	Emotional - Solar Plexus
☋ 16.5			20.6 ☋	Definition	Split Definition
☽ 53.5			6.4 ☽	Profile	3 / 5
☿ 34.1			19.5 ☿	Incarnation Cross	Right Angle Cross of Planning (37/40 | 9/16)
♀ 5.6			17.1 ♀	Signature	Satisfaction
♂ 43.6			60.3 ♂	Not-Self Theme	Frustration
♃ 37.4			36.3 ♃	Digestion	Calm
♄ 53.4			29.1 ♄	Sense	Meditation
♅ 50.5			28.1 ♅	Design Sense	Outer Vision
♆ 9.4			5.1 ♆	Motivation	Desire
♇ 18.6			18.6 ♇	Perspective	Power
⚷ 51.6			42.1 ⚷	Environment	Valleys

When we look at our charts, it's tempting to 'pick apart' the details and look at them separately. Much like the way our bodies work, and how every part of us and every cell is in communication with the entire body, our Human Design chart is our energetic blueprint, with all parts working together to create the story of our greatest potential and energy. Looking at the individual details can be helpful and also necessary; however, we always want to bring it back to the question 'Why would I be Designed this way?' and understand the overall theme as it relates to our life.

It's important to look at the entire story of the chart, and not just Type alone. For example, I'm a Manifesting Generator with five undefined Centres, a split definition, Emotional Authority and a lot of energetic themes of 'taking my time' and slowing down. You could look at another Manifesting Generator who has only two undefined Centres, a single definition, Sacral Authority and a lot of fast energy. If you only pay attention to the fact that we're both Manifesting Generators, you could put us into the same box energetically, but when you zoom out and look at the big picture, these two individuals are going to operate very differently from each other.

When I read someone's chart, what I'm really looking for are the themes, the story the chart tells and how the individual has actually been playing out these themes for their entire life.

Here's an example of how I might look at a chart, using my own as an example so you can see the story unfolding. (Remember that reading a chart takes practice; it's a skill that you'll cultivate over time, and it's really only necessary when you want to dive into the deepest elements of your chart or read other people's charts with confidence.)

TYPE – MANIFESTING GENERATOR

I'm a Manifesting Generator, but what makes that true? This is because I have a 'motor' – in my case a defined Sacral Centre, connected to the Throat Centre. This is a very fast energy, and as a Manifesting Generator, I have a tendency to move quickly and be very efficient, non-linear and multipassionate. This has proven to be very true throughout my life, as I've held several positions, started a few different businesses in different industries and I even know that Human Design itself isn't my final 'niche' or undertaking. I'm incredibly passionate about what I do, and I'm always dreaming up new ideas and ways to change the world.

STRATEGY – TO RESPOND

As a Manifesting Generator, I know that I am always in response to the world around me. There's no need for me to force anything or try to 'push' my way towards my dreams, because the Universe is always giving me things to respond to and taking me along my path. When I have a big idea, I simply write it down and then wait for something to respond to. My favourite example of this is with naming my podcast. Once upon a time, my podcast was not called The Human Design Podcast, it was called something else. I was in the shower one day, and I heard this voice say, 'You need to change the name of your podcast to

The Human Design Podcast', and this honestly shocked me. My impostor syndrome came running out like: *Who are you to do that?* The next day, I was on the phone to a mentor of mine and he said to me, 'You should do a Human Design podcast because there are no good podcasts out there about it.' Woah, there it was, my something to respond to! Even though I was terrified, I paid attention to the external cue and I changed the name and never looked back. I now have the leading global Human Design podcast.

AUTHORITY - EMOTIONAL

Because I have a defined Solar Plexus Centre, this makes me an Emotional Authority, which essentially is all about taking time to make decisions. Already, there's a paradox between that very quick Manifesting Generator energy and my Emotional Authority that needs to slow down. (This paradox shows up everywhere in my chart.) Before I learned Human Design, I resonated deeply with needing to take my time, especially with big decisions, and I've always felt uncomfortable with time pressure. Knowing that I'm an Emotional Authority gave me permission to reteach others how to treat me, using phrases like 'let me sleep on it' and 'I'll come back to you in a couple of days'. Yes, my energy works very quickly when I'm 'on', but I also need a balance of slowing down. Even my children understand this about me, and they often come to me with requests ahead of time and say, 'Mum, I'm asking you this now so you can think about it.'

PROFILE - 3 / 5

When I first came to Human Design, I was really disappointed that I was a Line 3. I've since come to love this about myself, but at first I viewed it as the 'difficult' Profile that always has to do things the hard way before working it out. As I deepened my understanding, I became friends with my Line 3 energy, knowing that my experiences are a huge part of my purpose and what I do in the world. People listen to and resonate deeply with me *because* of these experiences, and it's a big reason why my podcast was so successful even when I first started it – because I showed up and shared my experiences in a vulnerable way. My mantra for being a Line 3 is that 'I'm always winning or learning', and I know that there is no such thing as failure. This part of me needs to get out into the world, try things out, make a mess and then learn the lesson (and then share it with you).

The other part of my Profile is Line 5, rooted in wisdom and practical solutions. I know I'm here to heal, solve and lead, and use my experiences to help others. The Line 5 is also here to make an impact, which I've always felt deep inside me and it's what fuels my mission to make this work accessible to as many people as possible. In its shadow, the Line 5 can tend to be the 'saviour' and take on way too much responsibility for others, while putting themselves on the back burner. I've done my fair share of this in relationships, playing the role of the co-dependent and the people-pleaser. Human Design helped me understand just how important boundaries are for me as a Line 5, and even though I am always in service to others, I'm also now in service to myself so that I can lead and make an impact from an energetically sound place.

Looking at these Profile Lines put together, I understand that my purpose is to have experiences, go through trial and error, fall down, get up, make a mess, heal myself first and then take my experiences out into the world to help guide you with practical solutions and wisdom. My impact comes from my experiences and my ability to universalise them into resources that are tangible, actionable and simple (just like this book!).

THE BIGGER PICTURE

I could keep going for *pages* into the depths of my chart, but already we can see so many of the same themes and words coming up: balance, experience, impact and leadership. As you go through your own Design, I encourage you to pay attention to your own themes. What words come up over and over? What patterns keep playing out in your life? What do other people consistently see in you and ask you for?

This is how you start to harness the real power of your Design, when you let the story unfold and understand that you are perfectly Designed just as you are.

28.
CLOSING INVITATION

Congratulations, beautiful human. You've made it to the end of this book and equipped yourself with life-changing knowledge about how to live in the world as you were Designed to.

While there's no final exam waiting in these last few pages, you *are* in for the biggest test of your life: continuing your Human Design experiment beyond the pages of this book. The good news is that as long as you're taking Imperfect Action, this is a test you can't fail.

Everything that I've shared with you here in this book is an experiment for you to discover what is true for you, what Alignment feels like for you, and how you specifically express your Human Design so that you don't end up stuck at stage one. This material is here to help you create your life. The blueprint that Human Design provides only works when you step away from the paper and start to build something, trusting that you now have what you need to create what's meant for you.

Remember my own story: learning about my Design was only the first step. It wasn't all the *knowledge* that I gained about

Human Design that made me successful in every area of my life, it was the *implementation*. It was taking Imperfect Action. It was learning my Type, Strategy, Authority and Profile and then running the experiment of how my energy works. It was collecting the data, letting go of the things that were not true for me or that didn't work for me and then repeating and improving on the things that did.

And my experiment is far from over – I continue every day to take Imperfect Action and test out my Design so that I can stay in Alignment and keep moving towards fulfilment and authenticity as my life evolves.

Your experiment isn't over either – I hope it never will be. Because at the end of the day, we're all Designed to experiment: to continually move forward, continually discover ourselves, continually take active steps towards living a more aligned life.

You could even say that this journey that you're on right now *is* your purpose. The journey from feeling stuck, feeling scared, feeling out of Alignment, unhappy, broke or lonely towards taking continuous Imperfect Action in the direction of something better – *that* is your purpose, and all those negatives are calling you towards it. All the knowledge in this book, plus your active experimentation of it, *is* your purpose – the thing that will unlock the greatness, the potential in you, giving you the abundance, the happiness, the love, the purpose that you long for.

So, my friend, I will leave you with this simple question. Are you still in?

APPENDICES

APPENDIX I: DIVE DEEPER

This book is called *Human Design Made Simple*. It's a guide to transforming your life using Human Design without getting lost in the complexity of your chart.

Here's the thing, though: when you're *ready* – that is, once you've put everything you've learned from this book into action – diving deeper into all the rich complexity your chart has to offer can be really fun, deeply engaging and lead you in the direction of more transformational breakthroughs than you'll know what to do with.

After all, your Design is the imprint of the entire Universe upon you – a single individual, living in this moment in time . . . and the Universe and the experience of humanity can be a vastly, beautifully complicated thing. That means that some of the finer details of your Design are, quite simply, not so simple.

It's my belief and experience that you can successfully run your Human Design experiment based solely on the simple, straightforward elements we've covered in depth in this book: your Type, Strategy, Authority and Profile. The guidance offered by these elements is more than enough to help you step into the life you were Designed and deserve to live. Over time, Strategy and Authority alone will lead you to your most authentic self.

However, after spending the last 200 or so pages with me, you won't be surprised to learn that I also believe that living in

Alignment with your Human Design is an endlessly evolving experiment – one that always offers new opportunities for self-discovery and empowerment.

So why not dive deeper? Why not use everything you've learned so far – that simple, straightforward foundation – as a springboard for learning more about you, aligning more deeply with your Design and hitting the fast track for creating your dream life?

If continuing to work with the foundational elements of this book is what feels correct for you right now, trust that. Stop here with my full blessing and know that I'm so excited for you to play with the elements I've covered so far for as long as you need, to master them in your own time and transform yourself and your life at your own pace.

However, for those of you whose curiosity for Human Design has only just been piqued, I encourage you to take your experiment as far as feels correct for you. In the following pages I'll introduce you to some of the deeper, powerful elements you can add to your experiment, and send you in the direction of resources that can support you in your learning and your experiment.

GATES AND CHANNELS

On page 41, you learned about the Centres of the body, and how each of these Centres is the source of different energetic themes. Some of these Centres are defined for you, meaning that they are a consistent source of energy, and some of these Centres are undefined for you, meaning that they are *not* consistent sources of energy. But there's more to how energy flows through you than just which Centres are defined or undefined. There's a whole highway system of energy moving through you at any given time, and your Gates and Channels influence what specific energy moves and expresses itself through you.

GATES

Gates are the numbers you see inside your Centres on your chart. There are 64 Gates in Human Design – corresponding to the 64 Hexagrams of the I Ching, or the Chinese *Book of Changes* – and each Gate has a theme unique to it.

The Gates operate in the same way our genes do – they switch on and off and express differently depending on the environment.

In simple terms, the Gates are specific to superpowers, themes, gifts, talents and even values unique to you.

CHANNELS

Channels are the lines between the Centres on your chart; some are coloured in (defined) and others are not (undefined). When defined, they move the energy from Centre to Centre via the connection between two Gates. When Gates are connected by a Channel, a new energy or theme within your Design is revealed.

EXPERIMENTING WITH GATES AND CHANNELS

When you're ready to start learning about and experimenting with your Gates and Channels, check out this episode of my podcast:

www.emmadunwoody.com/blog/the-human-design-podcast-episode-270-hd-roadmap-part-9-gates-and-channels

And for even more information about the Gates, I highly recommend Richard Rudd's book, *The Gene Keys*. Rudd's work has been a constant companion on my own deep-dive into Human Design, and his ideas play a central role in my Transformational Human Design Model.

PLANETS

You may remember from the introduction that your Human Design chart is generated based on where the planets were in the sky at the time of your birth. That means that the location of the planets and other celestial bodies in the sky at the time of your birth, and approximately three months before you were born (this is when your soul enters the body, according to Human Design), imprinted their energies on you and your Design. As the planets, the moon and the sun move through the sky they continue to imprint their energy on you, affecting how different elements of your Design may function at different times (in Human Design, we refer to these movements as the Transits).

Your Design is based on a total of 26 planetary activations, 13 each on the Design and Personality positions (when you're looking at your chart, you will typically see 13 planets on the right side and 13 planets on the left side of the chart).

The planets on the right-hand side are called the Personality activations and represent your conscious personality; in other words, who you think you are.

The planets on the left-hand side are called the Design or Body activations and represent your soul's purpose or destiny.

EACH PLANET IS ASSOCIATED WITH A CERTAIN THEME:

- Sun = Personality Expression/Life Force

- Earth = Grounding/Balance

- Moon = Driving Force

- North Node = Future Direction/Environment

- South Node = Past Direction/Environment

- Mercury = Communication/Thinking

- Venus = Values/Sociology

- Mars = Immaturity/Energy Dynamics

- Jupiter = Law/Protection

- Saturn = Discipline/The Judge/Restraint

- Uranus = Unusualness/Chaos and Order/Science

- Neptune = Illusion/Art/Spirituality

- Pluto = Truth/Transformation/Psychology

- Chiron = The Wounded Healer/Core Wounds (not included on all Human Design charts; if it is, it will be the very bottom planet on either side)

When you're ready to start experimenting with your Planets, follow along with the regular Transits series on my podcast

www.emmadunwoody.com/blog

INCARNATION CROSS

Incarnation Cross identifies the job your energy is doing as you move through your life – whether you are conscious of it or not.

Your Incarnation Cross is made up of the Gates in your Personality Sun, Personality Earth, Design Sun and Design Earth (these are the numbers behind the decimal points in the first two boxes in each of the Personality and Design columns on your chart) – you will need the four numbers of these Gates in this order to know your exact Incarnation Cross. It is also a significant contributor to your purpose in this lifetime; it will give you a good understanding of who you are here to be and what you are here to do.

Your Cross is not something you have to consciously 'do', it is something you already are.

EXPERIMENTING WITH YOUR INCARNATION CROSS

When you're ready to start learning about and experimenting with your Incarnation Cross, check out this episode of my podcast:

www.emmadunwoody.com/blog/the-human-design-podcast-episode-268-the-human-design-roadmap-part-8-incarnation-cross-made-simple

FOUR ARROWS

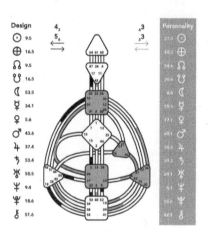

Often called the 'Variables' or 'Four Transformations', the Four Arrows on your chart offer additional detail on your unique experience of the world.

They can help you understand major and minor elements of how you move through daily life, and the guidance they provide will help you continue your experiment towards finding what feels correct and aligned for you. This includes information about your nutrition, environment, perspective, motivation, where you are more focused and where you are more receptive.

You'll find your arrows at the top right and left sides of your bodygraph on your chart.

EXPERIMENTING WITH YOUR FOUR ARROWS

When you're ready to start experimenting with your Four Arrows, check out this episode on my podcast:

www.emmadunwoody.com/blog/the-human-design-roadmap-part-10-the-4-arrows

APPENDIX II/BONUS MATERIAL: THE 64 GATES

In the following pages, you will find brief summaries for each of the 64 Gates in Human Design. This reference is based on a guide I created for members of my Human Design Community, HDX. You don't have to work with the Gates to run your Human Design experiment effectively, but learning about the Gates in your chart can help you deepen your understanding of your Design, tease out nuance and discover new themes that run through the elements of your chart. When – and if – you're ready to learn more about your Gates, you can turn to the summaries below as a reference about the overall themes associated with each Gate.

GATE 1 - THE CREATIVE

The Masculine. This is an energy that wants to create in a big way and with a unique style. It is an energy that wants to draw attention to itself. It fears having no creative energy, nothing to create and not being seen for its creativity.

GATE 2 - THE RECEPTIVE

The Feminine. This energy provides a deep knowing when you're heading in the correct direction for you. It attracts resources, and its highest potential is to let go and trust the path ahead as it unfolds, knowing it will always provide. It fears not having what it needs in life, so the mind tries to plan ahead and hustle for what it thinks it needs, instead of trusting the Universe to support and provide. The trick is to know how to receive.

GATE 3 - THE BEGINNING

This is the energy of creating calm and order from chaos. When you fear the chaos and/or change you cannot see the potential, strategy, order and path that is your natural talent. Allow the chaos to be potential for structure and innovation and you will fill in the steps as they present themselves – fear it and you will remain surrounded by chaos.

GATE 4 - SOLUTIONS

This is your natural drive to find answers, to keep investigating the question until you have all the answers and solutions. This Gate is a thinker and can be an *over*thinker. The mind fears not finding the answer, so it addictively overthinks in search of answers, but it is only when you allow the answer to drop in, to show itself to you in your calm, patient mind, that it will appear.

GATE 5 - FIXED RHYTHMS

This energy is purely rhythmic; it's the beat you move to each day. It loves the same habits and routines each day (for men) or each month (for women). Fear drives you to hurry and force your rhythm to fit in with or meet other people's expectations, but you must be patient with yourself and trust your own rhythm.

GATE 6 - CONFLICT

This energy wants to connect with others; it's looking to create intimacy in all kinds of relationships and to discover another person who will make a good match. When fear or frustration is present, the energy manifests as conflict, friction to break through and connect with the other.

GATE 7 - THE ARMY

This energy is the natural ability to lead and unite everyone in the same direction with a common purpose. However, if you lead before listening to where people want to go, then your leadership will not be powerful. In fear, this energy ignores what others want and dictates the direction for others. To be a great leader you must learn to listen first.

GATE 8 - CONTRIBUTION

This energy offers its own individual style and creativity to the world. Although others love to follow people with this energy, often they want to be left alone to do their own thing. In fear, they worry that being different will make them a target, weird or rejected, so instead they try to fit in, to be like everyone else, even though it eats them alive inside.

GATE 9 - FOCUS

This Gate has an ability to deeply focus on something; the challenge is that if it does not have a big and meaningful goal, then this focus will be used on the 'wrong' actions. If aligned to your big dream, your focus will be on the small actions that will get you there. Without that big, meaningful dream, your focus will keep you trapped in the small things that do not matter.

GATE 10 - SELF-LOVE

This is one of the energies of self-love and love for others. Often this is the lesson of learning to love and accept yourself as you are in each moment, and when you do, you influence others to do the same.

GATE 11 - IDEAS

This is the energy of creative flow. Ideas flow easily and often. The trap comes when you believe you have to put them all into action. Some ideas are for you, some are to give to others and some are just passing through. Follow your Strategy and Authority to know which ideas to put into action.

GATE 12 - CAUTION

This gate is all about the power you have to move people with your words. However, you must be in the mood for inspiration. When you are, then conversation and connection will flow easily, but if you're not in the mood, then your words may move people in the wrong direction.

GATE 13 - THE LISTENER

The energy of this gate makes others feel deeply safe to share their innermost stories, fears and trauma. You may be amazed at how quickly people share these things with you, but once they do, you keep them to yourself.

GATE 14 - POWER SKILLS

This is the energy of having unique skills. You successfully get paid for your individual gifts and receive good money for them. However, if you compromise and work the way others tell you to, then the money tap will be turned off.

GATE 15 - THE GATE OF EXTREMES

This energy is about the right timing. There is always the right time in nature – a time for birth, life, death and everything along that journey. You walk to your own beat, in your own timing and trust that even though it might not seem logical to others, it doesn't need to be as long as it feels correct to you.

GATE 16 - ENTHUSIASM

This is the energy of mastering more than one thing. It's the enthusiasm to develop mastery through repetition in more than one area.

GATE 17 - OPINIONS

This is the mental energy of opinions, the desire to share your own opinions from your life experience. This energy wants to be shared. However, don't get attached to your opinions, because by definition they are meant to change as you live and learn. Instead, be open to the possibility that what others have to share may change your opinion.

GATE 18 - CORRECTION

This is an ability to see the patterns that need to be upgraded to experience more joy in life, to experience the perfection found only in nature. Be aware that these corrections need to be invited. When not invited, they may not be received well by others.

GATE 19 - SENSITIVE

This is the energy of the sensitive, of people who are tuned in to the subtle energies and needs of all living things. You have a gift with animals and nature and can communicate with all life through frequency. Be aware that when in fear you will take care of other people's needs but not your own.

GATE 20 - THE NOW

This is the energy of having an awareness of the present moment and what lies within it. It is the ability to draw on the wisdom that is shared in the gap between the future and the past, thought and action. However, if you are too caught up in the mind, then you will miss the gift that is there for you in the present moment.

GATE 21 - THE HUNTER/HUNTRESS

This is the energy of being in control of your resources. You have a gift with money management and driving success. However, if you become controlling, you will drive those around you away.

GATE 22 - OPENNESS

This energy can easily work the room when in the mood. It's graceful, social and enchanting, with the ability to move people with their words. However, if not in the mood then your words can have the opposite effect just as quickly.

GATE 23 - ASSIMILATION

This energy takes your unique insights and translates them into language. It's the ability to take complex information and make it simple for others to receive. However, if you do not take the time to get your thoughts together before speaking, your communication will become unnecessarily complicated.

GATE 24 - RATIONALISATION

This is the energy to think about something over and over until you come to a new concept. Thinking identifies how to turn inspiration into action. However, don't get stuck in this repetitive thought pattern or it will keep you looping without progressing forever.

GATE 25 - SPIRIT

This is the energy of unconditional love, universal love and the higher self. You have the potential to be a powerful spiritual warrior, but you must surrender to spirit and not get trapped in the mind, wanting to convert everyone on your journey. Trust that everyone has unconditional love within them and they will find it in their own time.

GATE 26 - EGOIST

This is the energy to persuade others, and the ability to withstand others' rejection. Be careful that this energy does not turn into manipulation, but instead use your natural ability to pitch and persuade for genuine acts of service.

GATE 27 - NOURISHMENT

This energy is one of motherly support and nurturing, caring for the needs of the family or group. Be aware that you may forgo your own needs for nurturing and care if you use this gift to validate your self-worth in the family or group. You deserve nurturing and care whenever you need it.

GATE 28 - STRUGGLE

All humans are conditioned to think that we are here to struggle, but this energy shows us it is a choice. This Gate looks for greater meaning in the struggle and in doing so amplifies life from struggle to fulfilment.

GATE 29 - COMMITMENT

This is the energy of knowing what is correct for you to commit to and what is not. It may read as luck, but really it's the Universe giving you everything you need to make your commitment a reality. Be aware that you may find yourself saying 'yes' to too many things or to the wrong things to please others. This will lead to burnout over time, so learn to say 'no'.

GATE 30 - DESIRE

This is an emotional energy that wants to be expressed. It drives you to have emotional experiences, to fulfil its desires. It's all about timing; if you wait for the correct time, then you will have fulfilling emotional experiences.

GATE 31 - LEADERSHIP

This is the energy of the natural leader. You innately know the direction to go in and have a powerful voice to articulate it. However, this leadership must be democratic. Listen to where others want you to lead them before speaking, otherwise no one will follow you.

GATE 32 - CONTINUITY

This is the energy that drives you to constantly evaluate what you are focused on so that you can decide what needs to stay and what needs to go to move something towards success. You see the potential in people and whatever you are focused on. However, the fear of failure can prevent you from letting go or taking action. Remember there is no such thing as failure, only feedback.

GATE 33 - PRIVACY

This is the energy of a great listener, someone others seek out to share all their deepest secrets, fears and traumas with. They seek you out because you feel safe and they feel you will keep their secrets. You need your own retreat time – your privacy – in which to learn from and integrate all the stories that have been shared with you.

GATE 34 - POWER

This is the energy of the natural multitasker and multipassionate person. You have great power within you, which gives you the ability to do great things, to learn fast and integrate quickly. However, if you take on too many things, you will burn out and lose the magic ability you have to be extraordinary.

GATE 35 - CHANGE

This is the energy of being driven by restless curiosity and desiring to explore new horizons. This Gate drives you to share your experiences. You need to feel into your experiences, share and master them, gain wisdom from them and keep learning from them.

GATE 36 - CRISIS

This energy attracts emotional experiences that feel like crises. These experiences capture what it is to be human. You have a gift for resilience and can navigate challenges with a depth that is unmatched.

GATE 37 - FRIENDSHIP

This is the energy that wants equality for all people. You are the friend others feel drawn to and safe with. You have a knack for bringing together great communities. However, you need to feel equal within those communities or friendships, and that everything you put in is also received.

GATE 38 - THE FIGHTER

This energy brings the warrior within to the surface. The challenge is that this energy must be focused externally on something with great meaning, otherwise it will lead you to self-destruction.

GATE 39 - THE PROVOCATEUR

This is the energy of poking the bear to see what will happen, of provoking something. Provocation leads to experimentation, innovation and transformation. It's the energy of a child in a sandpit seeing if she can build her castle higher, wider and better. Be aware that provocation for no reason is no more than a smokescreen for your fear.

GATE 40 - ALONENESS

This is the energy of a person who loves their work and providing for the family/community/group. You have power that drives you to keep creating until your goals are made manifest. However, once this is done, you need time alone to recover.

GATE 41 - FANTASY

This is the energy of a dreamer, someone who has an active imagination and a talent for bringing their visions to life. Your imagination will lead you to some incredible experiences and empower others to dream big and believe in possibility. However, you must ground these fantasies in the world or risk getting lost in your mind and never making your dreams manifest.

GATE 42 - GROWTH

This energy understands when cycles should be repeated and when they should not. It's the ability to know what needs to be released and what needs to go around again to build upon. However, the mind may fear letting go because it views the end of a cycle as a death. Remember that in this death there is also a birth, and that is what this energy wants to bring forth.

GATE 43 - INSIGHT

This is a mental energy, one of insight, inspiration and break-through. It is experienced as a knowing in the moment. Your insights will lead you down a new path or way of doing and being. The more you listen, the more insights will come. However, if you ignore them, you will quickly become deaf to your insights altogether.

GATE 44 - PATTERNS

This is the energy to see the patterns that move the human race forward. You have a deep memory of the past and what did not work. You are intuitively guided to create better patterns so that we may move from surviving to thriving. Don't allow your mind to get stuck in the past; your gift is building our future.

GATE 45 - GATHERER

This Gate has the ability to accumulate great wealth. Whether it be abundance in your relationships, or financial, physical or emotional wealth, you are a natural leader and authority. You have a powerful voice for manifesting, so be careful what you speak about because it will manifest quickly.

GATE 46 - DETERMINATION OF THE SELF

This is the energy of being in the right place at the right time, and it requires you to listen to your body to identify when the timing feels right. Your energy is contagious when you're in Alignment, but if you are not listening to or following your body's guidance, you'll miss the serendipity and Universal guidance.

GATE 47 - REALISING

This is the energy of the 'aha moment'. This highly visual energy has passed down the patterns and karma of the generations before. You have the ability to process a great deal of mental information to help you eventually reach a realisation. If you pressure yourself for an answer, then the realisation will not come, so surrender to the process and allow realisation to drop in when it's ready.

GATE 48 - DEPTH

This is the energy of the depths within you. When you access them, you will have an abundance of solutions and wisdom to share, but you may also have a deep fear of what you might find within these depths. You fear that you are inadequate. This is not true – you have great depth that needs to be shared.

GATE 49 - REVOLUTION

This is the energy that upholds the principles within a relationship, family or group. You make sure others maintain the standards as well. However, when the principles no longer work or reflect the family/community, then it's time to start a revolution. You can be very black-and-white, leading you to walk away from a relationship or group prematurely.

GATE 50 - VALUES

This is the energy of instilling the right values in others. It's about family and societal conduct, the unwritten laws and rules of being a part of the family or community. You tend to take too much responsibility for ensuring others live up to these values.

GATE 51 - SHOCK

This is the energy of shock, which serves the purpose of waking others up. You often will not understand why others are shocked by your words, but it is because your energy is moving them into a higher consciousness. You may find that you are competitive with others or they are with you, but do not let this cloud your own unique path.

GATE 52 - STILLNESS

This is the energy of stillness and the guidance that comes to you within the stillness. This is not about being inactive, but being deeply and actively still – like a meditation master. You have a unique ability to sit in stillness and concentration, but make sure you are concentrating on the correct things to progress towards your dreams.

GATE 53 - BEGINNINGS

This is the energy of new beginnings. It guides you to know which things to begin and expand with great power. When you make your choice from love and not from fear, then you can be unstoppable. However, if you choose fear, you will begin many things but never expand any of them.

GATE 54 - AMBITION

This is the energy of following your ambition and allowing it to guide you to great success and fulfilment. You have the ability to succeed at the things that have meaning for you. Be aware that if you allow your ambition to drive your greed, then you may have money but you will feel deeply unfulfilled.

GATE 55 - ABUNDANCE

This is the energy of true abundance. This Gate offers the freedom to be you and attract abundance in all good things. You are a moody person – riding the emotional wave is a big part of life. When you surrender to your true spirit, you will find beauty in all emotions you experience.

GATE 56 - STIMULATION

This is the energy of the storyteller. It drives you to share the ideas and experiences that have been told to you. You need balance between being under- and overstimulated.

GATE 57 - INTUITION

This is the energy of the intuitive. The more you listen to and act on your intuition, the louder it gets. With practice, you will be given images of the future. However, if you fear the future, then your gift will not reach its greatest potential.

GATE 58 - JOY

This is the energy of correcting anything that is standing in the way of beauty and joy. It's an energy of well-being. Your energy is very attractive to others and you love to be full of vitality. Joy and beauty are vital for you to thrive; do not diminish the importance of these qualities to you.

GATE 59 - INTIMACY

This is the energy of intimacy in relationships. It is the life force energy that brings two people together. You need to take your time to know if you trust a relationship; you may have a mistrust of relationships from rushing the process in the past. You are magnetic and you can get caught up in romantic moments, but you need to slow down and allow intimacy to grow organically.

GATE 60 - LIMITATION

This is the energy of breaking through percieved limits. When you think you have blocks and lack opportunity or resources, you will be driven to surpass your limitations. Do not impose limitations on yourself; instead ask how your perceived limitations can help you succeed.

GATE 61 - MYSTERY

This is the energy to uncover universal truths, to question everything and to discover the mysteries of our Universe. You want to know yourself, and all of life, at its deepest level. This truth-seeking can cause you to lose your connection to reality, so be sure to ground what you discover in your real life.

GATE 62 - DETAIL

This is the energy that can name, concretise and communicate visual patterns. You organise details as facts to understand and explain complex concepts. These concepts need to be created with an open and flexible mind that is willing to improve upon them when more detail is received, otherwise you will get stuck on the unimportant details.

GATE 63 - DOUBT

This is the energy that identifies inconsistency and weakness in the patterns that move life forward. This ability can create doubt in your mind because you know there is a better way. It can take time to discover the better way, and the process needs to happen in its own time. Watch out for the self-doubt that may creep in when you are yet to concretise new patterns.

GATE 64 - CONFUSION

This is the energy of giving the huge amounts of universal information that you receive time to drop in and make sense. You have the capacity to comprehend large amounts of information, but if you feel pressured to make sense of it before you're ready, then confusion will prevail.

ACKNOWLEDGEMENTS

This book has been a gift to write, and I feel so supported by some brilliant people. My friend Jenni Crowther for being the serendipitous initiator of this dream. Jane Graham Maw and Amy O'Shea who helped me get my book deal, Sam Jackson and your team at Ebury who brought it into being.

Chelsea Pippin who was incredible in bringing my extensive content together so we could turn it into this book, your support and expertise in the entire process was brilliant, thank you for co-parenting this book baby with me.

Amanda Foley, my PR director and friend. Thank you for being your brilliant self and making sure this book gets shared everywhere worldwide.

Taylor my COO and dearest friend, for always managing all the details (and me) so we can create something extraordinary, and my entire team for being so incredible.

My boys Cooper and Oscar, my great loves, thank you for choosing me and inspiring me to be the best me I can be. May the contents of this book continue to empower you to live a free and authentic life.

INDEX

Note: page numbers in **bold** refer to diagrams.

ABOUT THE AUTHOR

Emma Dunwoody is a Human Design expert, Master Coach, behavioural specialist and host of the #1 Global Human Design Podcast. She wakes people up to the power within them using her unique method of Transformational Human Design™, a system of self-knowledge and guidance unlike anything else that exists. Her vision is to take Human Design mainstream so it becomes more widely accepted than any other global profiling, behavioural or healing system–she believes it will transform personal development, education and business forever.